SPRING 61

A JOURNAL OF
ARCHETYPE
AND
CULTURE

Spring, 1997

SPRING PUBLICATIONS

WOODSTOCK, CONNECTICUT 06281

ACKNOWLEDGMENTS

To Princeton University Press for quotations from the *Collected Works (CW)* of C. G. Jung (Bollingen Series XX), translated by R. F. C. Hull, edited by H. Read, M. Fordham, G. Adler, and Wm. McGuire, and published in Great Britain by Routledge and Kegan Paul, London. Other quotations have been acknowledged throughout in appropriate notes and references.

Spring is the oldest Jungian journal in the world. It was founded in 1941 by the Analytical Psychology Club of New York. In 1970, James Hillman transferred its editing and publication to Zürich, Switzerland. From 1978 to 1988, it was edited in Dallas, Texas. Since 1988 it has been edited in Connecticut.

Contents

HAITI OR THE PSYCHOLOGY OF BLACK: Editors' Note

JAMES HILLMAN
The Seduction of Black 1

STEPHEN DIGGS
Alchemy of the Blues 16

JUDI BERTOIA
Colour as Language and Symptom 51

HENRY HOGARTH
The Garden and the Gods:
Life from the Haitian Perspective 61

CLAUDINE MICHEL
Teaching Haitian Vodou 83

DIANNE SKAFTE
The Sibyls: Bridging Personal Identity
and Oracular Knowing 100

JOHN E. BURNS
A Twelve Step Meeting of the Afro-Brazilian Gods 113

Michael Ortiz Hill
C. G. Jung in the Heart of Darkness   125

Sheila Grimaldi-Craig
Going Black (book review)   134

Book Reviews   144

SPRING 61: HAITI OR THE PSYCHOLOGY OF BLACK

Certain questions keep appearing in one form or another in several of the papers in this issue: Is there (to be) a psychology of black? And is it (would it be) the same as a psychology of black people? And who (blacks or whites or both?) will (should) (could) articulate such a psychology?

Loaded questions! Just about everyone agrees that a psychology of black would not be a psychology of race (or "race," as Michael Vannoy Adams insists in his new book, handling that impossible word only with the forceps of quotation marks). It would be a psychology of color(s). (The plural is necessary because as soon as you start talking black, you seem to be talking the blues, too.)

We present this issue of Spring as a small contribution to the drafting of such a psychology. It is far from being anything complete. We did not recruit these papers or commission them for this task—like all issues of Spring the papers just seem to come in as always at random but then more and more on a single theme until one day our editors wake up and realize they have the makings of an issue.

But better such incompleteness, we think, than the total neglect of the subject of black psychology on the part of our Jungian forebears (not to mention Freudian and others). Jung, of course, did have a lot to say on the subject of black people, as more than one of our authors here note. But what he had to say seems so...white. It is white psychology considering where black people fit into white fantasies and fears.

For a black psychology to speak for itself, it will have to do more than merely adapt the framework of a white psychology. (We're talking an archetypal black psychology here, brothers and sisters, in case you forgot—and if it's archetypal, it will have its own (divine) voice(s), its own look and feel, its own fears and fantasies).

This is why we think Haitian mythology is so important to the subject at hand, because the Haitians are virtually the last polytheistic people on the planet whose psyches are bathed in a truly black psychology (with both a light and a dark version). They really do think differently. They see differently.

Of course John Burns would include Brazil in a similar scope; writing of his experiences with alcoholics in that country, he points out how "unlike Haiti, the Afro-Brazilian religions thrive in the metropolis." His own Twelve Step program in San Paulo uses all the gods in the Brazilian pantheon. (A white psychology's program, a black psychology's psyche?)

The point is, this is not a monolith, a universality, a single-mindedness, this articulation of the psychological. The gods are not the same all over the planet. Nothing could be more wrong—or more white?—than to treat psychology as the application of formulas, of fixed principles and programs out of Zürich or Vienna or New York. A psychology of black is not going to come out of those places any more than it's going to come out of M.I.T. or Harvard. It's going to come out of Haiti or a similar state of mind.

And having declared that, we would like to dedicate this issue of *Spring* to one of the most distinguished members of our Advisory Board. Poet and critic Selden Rodman, now eighty-seven, was the prime instigator of the magnificent Haitian art renaissance that bloomed in the 1940s. He helped found the Haitian Art Center in Port-au-Prince, providing art materials to all who wanted to try their hand at picturing or sculpting the images of the Haitian psyche, but offering absolutely no instruction or Western orientation, so that everything produced was self-taught, originally imagined, ground-breakingly fresh. The results are now legendary, and can be seen in dozens of books (including his own magisterial *Where Art Is Joy*) as well as on the walls of every serious art museum in the world.

His was one of the first steps toward articulating a psychology of black, and we are indeed proud that his name is on the masthead of this particular issue of *Spring*. To Selden!

— The Editors

The Seduction of Black

JAMES HILLMAN

"The principle of the art is the raven..."

—C. G. Jung, *CW* §14, 36

I. The Color of Non-Color

Black and White. These two non-colors to the Newtonian eye of science are, to the eye of culture, the first of all colors—the truly primary colors.

Two University of California ethnologists published a survey of the words for colors in some ninety-eight languages.[1] From this base they make a wider, universal claim. They report that all languages have terms for black and white, dark and light, obscure and bright. Then, second, they report that if a language has a third color term, it is universally red, and if a fourth and fifth, it is universally yellow or green, followed by blue, sixth, brown seventh, and so on, a scale that operates almost without exception in their collection of diverse languages.

James Hillman is the Senior Editor of this journal. Parts of this paper were first read in the inaugural evening of "The Colors of Life Conference and Festival" in Torino, Italy, in August, 1995.

For us, their principal finding and the one least contested by others is the primacy of the black-white pair. All cultures, it seems, make this distinction, suggesting both the importance of the diurnal rhythm,[2] and particularly for psychology, suggesting that contrast is essential to consciousness.

Among sub-Saharan African peoples, the three primary colors — black-white-red (and I am translating more metaphorically concrete expressions into our abstract color terms) — form the very ruling principles of the cosmos. They are not merely color words, names of hues.

We find a similar idea in the three *gunas* in Indian cosmology: black *tamas*, red *rajas*, and white *sattva* enter into the composition of all things. The deservedly authoritative anthropologist Victor Turner states that these three colors "provide a primordial classification of reality."[3] They are not merely perceptual qualities, but as "experiences common to all mankind" they are like archetypal "forces," "biologically, psychologically and logically prior to social classifications, moieties, clans, sex totems, and all the rest." For culture, black and white, and red, precede and determine the way human life is lived. Turner's claim further separates the culture of color from the science of color. From the cultural viewpoint colors are not mere secondary qualities, reducible to physical sensations in neurological systems in the subjective perceiver. On the one hand colors have to do with light, reflection, optics and nerves; on the other hand, they have something to do with the world itself. They are the world itself, and this world is not merely a colored world as if by accidents of light and chemistry, or as if decorated by a painterly God. Colors present the world's phenomenal actuality, the way the world shows itself, and, as operational agents in the world, colors are primary formative principles. Even the rainbow derives its colors from the phenomenal world (rather than from the refraction of light) according to the medieval imagination: "From the heavens it derives the fiery color; from water, the purple; from air, the blue; and from the earth the grassy color."[4] Whether the earth takes its colors from an invisible colorless light above or composes that light by means of its own elemental hues (e.g., green grass, blue water, etc.), the rainbow joins visible and invisible. Torah says God set forth the rainbow as a visible sign that the cosmos is sustained by invisible principles. The rainbow also declares the double principle that the display of beauty goes hand in hand with discrimination, the spectrum of finely differentiated hues.

Only in a physically reduced world view, i.e., a world view reduced to and by physics, can black be called a non-color, an absence of color, a deprivation of light. This privative definition of black ignores the fact that black appears in broad daylight in naturally given pigments and in other phenomena from charcoal and obsidian to blackberries and animal eyes.

Moreover, the negative and privative definition of black promotes the moralization of the black-white pair. Black then is defined as not-white, and is deprived of all the virtues attributed to white. The contrast becomes opposition, even contradiction, as if day would be defined as non-night, and a blackberry be defined as a non-whiteberry.

The law of contradiction when moralized gives rise to our current Western mind-set, beginning in the 16th and 17th centuries, the Age of Light, where God is identified with whiteness and purity, and black, with the *privatio boni*, becoming ever more strongly the color of evil.

Northern European and American racism may have begun in the moralization of color terms. Long before any English speaking adventurer touched the shores of West Africa, fifteenth-century meanings of "black" included: "deeply stained with dirt; soiled; dirty, foul; malignant, atrocious, horrible, wicked; disastrous, baneful, sinister..." When the first English-speaking sailors spied natives on West African shores, they called these people "black." That was the first generally descriptive term they used—not naked, not savage, not pagan, but black. Once named, these Native peoples carried all the meanings implied in that term. The English term "white" to characterize an ethnic group first occurs in 1604, after the perception of Africans as "black." The moralization and opposition between white and black continues to this day in general English-language usage as white equals good, black equals bad, dirty, foul, sinister, evil, etc. White as a term for Christians became firmly established by 1680 in the American language.

The disdain for black is not only contemporary, Western and English. The color black in the Greek world, and in African languages also, carried meanings contrasting with white and red, and included not only the fertility of the earth and the mystery of the underworld, but also disease, suffering, labor, sorcery and bad luck.

Black, however, is no more cursed than any other color. Color terms bear extremely contrary meanings. Each is weighted down with a composite of opposites—yellow as sunshine and decay; green with hope and envy; blue with puritanism and prurience; etc. The curse of black comes only when color terms are laid onto human beings, a curse of our Anglo-American culture and, as I've tried elsewhere at length to explain,[5] that has cursed the majority culture by labeling it white, thereby loading it with the archetypal curse of white supremacy.

Could there be an archetypal aspect to darkness that might account for our disdain, as well as the fear, the physiological shudder it can release? Does the human eye prefer light to darkness? Is the human being heliotropic, fundamentally adapted to light? Is visual perception its preferred sense as we witness in the embryo, where from its earliest weeks the rudimentary optical system begins to form before many others?

If the human animal has an innate predilection to light, then the exclusion of black as a color term substituting for "darkness" might find justification. The exclusion of darkness favors adaptation to the phenomenal world and optimal functioning within it by means of our primary organs of sense, the eyes. Then we might simplistically conclude that the definition of black as a non-color belongs to the ocular identity of human consciousness. The eye becomes the *pars pro toto* for habitual human consciousness, and black threatens the very core of this identity. This threat is also its virtue.

II. The Alchemical Nigredo

The cosmic significance of these three primary colors appear as well in early Western science, that is, in the tradition of alchemy. Of the three, black plays an especially important role, as the base of the work, and even enters into the formation of the word alchemy. The root *khem* refers to Egypt as the black land, or land of black soil, and the art of alchemy was called a "black" art or science. The Western alchemical tradition traces its source to the *techne* of Egyptian embalming, dyeing of cloth, jewelry, and cosmetics.

The first four color terms—black, white, red and yellow—are also the primary color terms embracing the entire alchemical opus—nigredo, albedo, xanthosis or citrinitas and rubedo. These color terms describe a) the stages of the work, b) conditions of the material worked on, and c) states in the psyche of the artifex or worker-alchemist. Each color term combines three distinct categories which our modern consciousness keeps separate: the mode of working, the stuff worked on, and the condition of the worker. For our epistemology there is no inherent or necessary relation between method, problem and subjectivity.

For example, for any substance to enter the nigredo phase and blacken, then the operations must be dark and are called in alchemical language: mortificatio, putrefactio, calcinatio, iteratio, etc. That is, the *modus operandi* is slow, repetitive, difficult, desiccating, severe, astringent, effortful, coagulating and/or pulverizing. All the while the worker enters a nigredo state: depressed, confused, constricted, anguished, and subject to pessimistic, even paranoid, thoughts of sickness, failure and death.

The alchemical mode of science maintained the law of similitudes between all participants in any activity: the work, the way of working and the worker. All must conform; whereas we can have a science in which the subjectivity of the experimenter may be radically separated from the experimental design and from the materials of the experiment.

Our science seeks universality of experimental design that can be used by any worker, anywhere, on any problem. Statistics are essential to it. Alchemical method treats each problem by each alchemist according both to its nature and his or her nature. That is why no comprehensive system can be drawn from alchemical texts; why measurement plays an indifferent role; why the inventions of each alchemist are stridently opposed by other alchemists; and why even the materials worked on are so radically differentiated—so many kinds of salt, so many names for mercury, so many styles and shapes of instruments.

The radical idiosyncrasy and yet deep concordance between method, problem and subjectivity also accounts for why depth psychology finds alchemy so useful a background for the work in its laboratories: the consulting rooms where nigredo conditions are all too familiar.

We may read this conformity between worker, the worked on and way of working, backwards, offering psychological insights that cannot be gained from a Cartesian-Newtonian science which separates worker from the work. From alchemy we learn that if you, as a worker in any field on any project—from research to marriage, from business to painting—become exhausted, dried out, stuck, depressed and confused, then you have indications of a nigredo phase and the material you are encountering is itself dark and obstinate. This "depression" signifies a failure neither of your personality nor of your method. In fact the very difficulties in your method and the darkness of your fantasies indicate that you are in the right place and doing the right thing just because of the darkness.

The optimistic and more Christianized readings of alchemical texts give to the nigredo mainly an early place in the work, emphasizing progress away from it to better conditions when blackness will be overcome and a new day of the albedo will resurrect from obfuscation and despair. Christianized readings seem unable to avoid salvationalism.[6]

This is only one possible reading. The texts make very clear that the nigredo is not identical with the *materia prima*, a much larger basket of conditions. The nigredo is not the beginning, but an accomplished stage. Black is an achievement! It is a condition of something having been worked upon, as charcoal is the result of fire acting on a naive and natural condition of wood, as black feces is the result of digested blood, as blackened fungus is the result of putrefaction and decay. Although depression, fixations and obsessions, and a general blackening of mood and vision, may first bring a person to therapy, these conditions indicate that the soul is already engaged in its opus. The psychological initiation began before therapy's first hour. Jung says of the nigredo, "the major opus begins at this point" [*CW* 14, §708].

III. Black Intentions

What does black intend to achieve? Why is it an accomplishment? Let me briefly list what blackening performs, without using the mystical language of John of the Cross, Simone Weil and other proponents of religious darkness. First, as non-color, black extinguishes the perceptual colored world.

Second, the blackening negates the "light," whether that be the light of knowledge, the attachment to solar consciousness as far-seeing prediction, or the feeling that phenomena can be understood. Black dissolves meaning, and the hope for meaning. We are benighted.

Third, the two processes most relevant for producing blackness—putrefaction and mortification—break down the inner cohesion of any fixed state. Putrefaction by decomposition or falling apart; mortification by grinding down, as seeds in a mortar are refined into ever thinner and smaller particles. Newton himself wrote: "For the production of black the Corpuscles must be less than of any of those which exhibit Colours."[7]

This "subtle dissolver" when mixed into other hues brings about their darkening and deepening, or in alchemical psychology's language, their suffering. Black steers all varieties of brightness into the shade. Is corruption black's intention?

An answer depends on what is meant by "shade." Surely, this

intention is not merely the sullying of innocence, the staining of the only natural, that necessary preliminary to all alchemical thinking. So, we are not dealing merely with the corruption of natural innocence. The "shade" that black afflicts pertains to the deeper and invisible realm of shades, the Kingdom of Hades who is the ultimate "subtle dissolver" of the luminous world.

The thickness and solidity of the materials he worked with, Newton said, became more attenuated by fire and by putrefaction, "the more subtle dissolver." Black matter was the least formed and the most susceptible to dissolution, or in our language, chaos.

We can begin to see—through a glass darkly—why the color black is condemned to be a "non-color." It carries the meanings of the random and the formless. Like a black hole, it sucks into it and makes vanish the fundamental security structures of Western consciousness.

By absenting color, black prevents phenomena from presenting their virtues. Black's deconstruction of any positivity—experienced as doubt, negative thinking, suspicion, undoing, valuelessness—explains why the nigredo is necessary to every paradigm shift.

Black breaks the paradigm; it dissolves whatever we rely upon as real and dear. Its negative force deprives consciousness of its dependable and comforting notions of goodness. If knowledge be the good, then black confuses it with clouds of unknowing; if life be the good, then black stands for death; if moral virtues be the good, then black means evil. If nature is conceived as a many-colored splendor, then black signifies the entire *opus contra naturam*, translating the great phenomenal world into the inked abstractions of letters, numbers and lines, replacing the palpable and visual given with the data of marks and traces. By deconstructing presence into absence, the nigredo makes possible psychological change.

Therefore, each moment of blackening is a harbinger of alteration, of invisible discovery and of dissolution of attachments to whatever has been taken as truth and reality, solid fact or dogmatic virtue. It darkens and sophisticates the eye so that it can see through. Thus black often becomes the color of dress for the underworld, urban sophisticates and the old who have seen a lot.

Because black breaks the comforting paradigms, it is the color preferred by the spiritually driven and politically pressuring reformers and "outsiders"—adolescents, rebels, pirates, ladies of the night, cultists, bikers, satanists, puritans, anarchists, hitmen, priests—all the "non-conformistas" who then become trapped by their own identification with black, confusing a stage of being with a state of being.

Though alchemical maxims say the work must resemble a "raven's head" in its blackness and that this raven is "the principle of the art," these sayings identify the depth of black's radicality. They do not intend radical identity or identification with black. Black is itself not a paradigm but a paradigm breaker. That's why it is placed as a phase within a process of colors, and why it appears again and again in life and work in order to deconstruct (*solve et coagula*) what has become an identity. Those who wear the blackshirt and the black-robe, the black hood and the black undergarments as signs of radical identity become thereby neither anarchists, outsiders nor reformers, but fundamentalists. Hence, the rigid severity and monotheistic literalism of revolutionaries.

Alchemical psychology teaches us to read as accomplishments the fruitlessly bitter and dry periods, the melancholies that seem never to end, the wounds that do not heal to the status quo ante, the grinding sadistic mortifications of shame and the putrefactions of love and friendships. These are beginnings because they are endings, dissolutions, deconstructions. But, they are not the beginning, as a one-time-only occurrence. Such would be a literal reading of the alchemical process which is not a unidirectional model, progressing in time. It is an *iteratio*; black repeats in order for the deconstruction to continue, as shown for instance by Figure Nine of Jung's commentary on the alchemical Rosarium [CW 16, §285]. The soul returns, the king and queen are joined—yet out of the ground emerge the dark birds.

I do not wish to leave you in this black state, as if I were a Savanarola preacher, or a transalpine Lutheran, or a Biblical

Jeremiah. I want neither to condemn you to blackness nor relieve you from it by promising the return of the colored world which alchemical psychology presents in gorgeous images.

IV. "Blacker than Black"

I am moved by another intention: to warn. And warning, too, belongs to the nigredo for it speaks with the voice of the raven, foretelling dire happenings that may result from the seduction of black. Remember how 19th-century colonials feared going black, how Joseph Conrad perceived a madness and a horror in the heart of darkness, how the black plague, the black knight, the black shirt and the black inquisitor haunt European history as the black-clothed puritan haunts American, and that many of the scariest images of childhood, from chimney sweep, witch, magician and batman, the Rotweiler and the Doberman, to skeletons in the *danse macabre* and the grim reaper himself, stalk the halls of fantasy—all in black. To socialize these fears into race relations does not get at the archetypal imagination of these fears.

Let's be clear: Negro is not nigredo, though a figure in a dream called "black," as any dream phenomenon so named, may usher in and represent the blackening. But especially in a racist society we must keep very distinct the epithets that arbitrarily and viciously color human beings on the one hand and, on the other, cosmic forces that shape the soul apart from human beings. What we fear is black magic: the magical pull of black attraction, the soul's desire to descend into darkness, like Persephone unto Hades.[8] We fear what we most desire and desire what we most fear.

The essence of this fear lies in the black radix itself: that it is implacable, indelible, permanent, a crucial component of the aqua permanens—that sense of psychic reality underlining and underlying all other realities, like an awareness of death.

Thus the tragic paradox of black. It sticks like tar to its own selfsame negativity. As it curses other colors by darkening their brightness, it curses itself as well by making itself "blacker than black,"

THE SEDUCTION OF BLACK 11

beyond the touch of Mercurius duplex.

In other words, the color required for change deprives itself of change, tending to become ever more literal, reductive and severe. Of all alchemical colors, black is the most densely inflexible and therefore the most oppressive and dangerously literal state of soul. Hence clinicians fear that nigredo conditions of depression will lead to literal suicide, revengeful anger to violence, and hatred to domestic cruelty. Hence, too, reductive moves and "shadow" work in therapy feel so concrete and confining.

Of course, as painters know, there are many saturations of black. Part of the painter's opus is the differentiation of blacks—blacks that recede and absorb, those that dampen and soften, those that etch and sharpen, and others that shine almost with effulgence—a *sol niger*. Nonetheless, the alchemical maxim "blacker than black" states an ultimate radicality beyond all different shades and varieties. What is blacker than black is the archetypal essence of darkness itself, at times named by alchemy, night, satan, sin, raven, chaos, tenebrositas, black dog, death...

Since Mercurius is hidden and the albedo an unpredictable grace, what can "cure" the nigredo? What can release the soul from its somber identification? This is the question posed in every analysis, and posed during the nigredo moments of every life. The alchemist answer: decapitation.

According to Jung [*CW* 14, §730], the black spirit is to be beheaded, an act which separates understanding from its identification with suffering. Because "in the nigredo the brain turns black" [*ibid.* §733], decapitation "emancipates the cogitatio." Blackness remains; it is not done away with; you are not rid of it. You are, however, delivered from identity with it. The distinction between head and body creates a two, while suffering imprisons you in singleness. Decapitation allows the mind to recognize and thereby be freer from what the body feels.

Of course, decapitation makes sense as an operation only as a treatment for the nigredo. It is, of course, contraindicated—even redundantly senseless—for those conditions of soul where the head is barely attached and rarely recognizes anything the body feels. And, of course, this alchemical "body" refers not merely to the physical flesh and its symptoms, but to all imaginal perspectives that are trapped in habitual concretisms.

Decapitation is therefore a *separatio*—to use an alchemical term for the basic therapeutic move of making distinctions, or analyzing. Despite the fixity of nigredo moods and their repetitious thoughts, analysis separates the material—dreams, moods, projections, symptoms—from the mind's literal identification with this material. The dense and oppressive material becomes images that can be entertained by the mind. Mental images emancipate us from slavery to the nigredo; though the material remains dark, decapitation allows the mind to cogitate the darkness.

Alchemy advises "beware of the physical in the material." It is not the material of suffering that poisons the work with despair, but the physical, that is, the substantive naturalistic mind that prevents an imaginative appreciation of the material. Just this imaginative appreciation is what alchemical psychology offers. Patients, and any of us at many times, who are "unable to imagine" are often trapped in the nigredo by past traumata, and caught by the "physical in the material." These same patients, however, may be trapped as well in the nigredo of their therapists who have not been decapitated and whose cogitations have not been emancipated from reductive, naturalistic and literal understanding of what's going on.

Literalism is surely the most obdurate of all our habitual concretisms. By this "literalism" I mean singleness of meaning. I mean identification of any concrete embodiment with its "word," that identity between word and thing so that words become things. Decapitation also frees the word "black" from only nigredo meanings, therewith freeing those called "Black" from the indelible fixities of nigredo projections.

Remember here that the "word" in our culture is inked in black, and this selection of color for ink may be more than merely convenient and efficient. The very blackness of the inked letter supports its indelible fixity and abets the cursing power of literalism.

Perhaps, then, the contemporary attempts at multiple meanings (polysemousness), of separating the signifier and the signified, of playing with the ambiguity of "trace," troping, displacing, and insisting upon difference and, as well, the absenting of all certitudes from positive propositions—these deconstructive moves may be French modes of decapitating the *cogito,* that is, freeing the mind from the singleness that I condemn as literalism. The entire French effort may be alchemy-like attempts (the arcane obscurantism of deconstructive talk sounds indeed like the language of the alchemists) to invite Mercurius duplex back into the discourse from which French logical clarity had excused him.

Although I can grasp an alchemical intention in contemporary French thought, I do not profess its method: it stops short and remains an exercise of the *cogitatio.* The guillotine blade never quite cuts through. The brain remains blackened, and so the cogitations of its mind are read by critics as nihilism, Euro-pessimism, cynicism, negative theology and the latest fashion in existential despair, and therefore deconstructionism becomes one more habitual concretism of Western thought.

It stops short before the nigredo turns blue. After the black comes the blue—not cynical, but sad; not hard and smart, but slow. The blues bring the body back with a revisioned feeling, head and body rejoined. The alchemists spoke of this as the *unio mentalis* which I have tried to elaborate in an earlier essay.[9] As I say there, blue gives voice to the nigredo, and voice unites head and body. Darkness imagined as an invisible light, like a blue shadow, behind and within all things.

The principal concretism against which this present paper has been contending is the Newtonian convention that excludes black from the realm of color because it is not concretely visible in the spectrum. Perhaps, however, the fault is not Newton's at all, but results from black's cursed literalism, its archetypal desire to be outside this world, in the underworld of invisibilities, or in the dark kingdom of death. Perhaps, black cannot lift the curse from off its own head so that it becomes our job, each of us, to decapitate the nigredo, to emancipate our minds in a post-Newtonian manner.

For me, this emancipation of the mind means more than thinking dark thoughts with a blackened brain or suffering the body's profound depressions. It means the incorporation of invisibility within all perceptions, never losing the dark eye or ignoring the soul's desire for shades and sorrows. To be benighted is only the beginning; to be black, to see black—that's how the nigredo inescapably affects us. But, to see by means of black, to see the habitual as mystery, the apparent as ambiguous, shifts concretistic fixities into metaphorical images. This is the emancipation of the nigredo from literalism. Like cures like; we cure the nigredo by becoming, as the texts say, blacker than black, that is, archetypally black, and thereby no longer colored by all-too-human prejudices of color.

Becoming blacker than black would also bear upon the chaos and tragedy of what are misnamed "race" relations and are more truly color relations, because they are reflections in the human sphere of alchemical processes whose intentions only peripherally concern people. For the desire of alchemy was not merely toward the human soul; it sought the soul of the world. Alchemy is a cosmological work; to follow an alchemical psychology at once leads to working with the world. Alchemy would re-animate the dense and the neglected, sometimes called "matter," and alchemy demands an ever-returning descent into that darkness, that invisibility, sometimes called Hades.

By continuing to regard black as a non-color and segregating it from the bright beauty of the Newtonian spectrum, our faulty cosmology remains unable to find a place for the nigredo except as "shadow" phenomena such as crime, cruelty, racism, imprisonment, toxicity, and the mental disorder of depression. Also, our science, by locating nigredo phenomena only in subjectivity as human moods and human failures, continues its delusional method that disconnects the work from the worker and from the ecological world worked on.

Worse is the danger that our Western epistemology loses its ability to correct its own bright blindnesses by making radical paradigm shifts. The conversion of black from non-color to color is therefore not merely an issue of societal reform regarding the inclusion of darker peoples and darker shades of existence. The inclusion of black among the colors becomes a way Western consciousness might break the naive fundamentalism of its hopefully-colored illusions.

Notes

[1] Brent Berlin and Paul Kay. *Basic Color Terms: Their Universality and Evolution.* Berkeley: Univ. of California Press, 1969.
[2] Gilbert Durand. *Les structures anthropologiques de l'Imaginaire.* Paris: Presses Univ. France, 1963.
[3] Victor Turner. *The Forest of Symbols.* Ithaca: Cornell UP, 1967.
[4] Carl B. Boyer. *The Rainbow, From Myth to Mathematics.* Princeton: Princeton UP, 1987.
[5] *Cf.* James Hillman. "Notes on White Supremacy," *Spring 1986.* Dallas: Spring Publications, 1986. This article provides a fuller treatment of the racial implications of color terms.
[6] *Cf.* Edward F. Edinger. *Anatomy of the Psyche: Alchemical Symbolism in Psychotherapy.* LaSalle, Ill.: Open Court, 1985.
[7] B. J. T. Dobbs. *The Foundations of Newton's Alchemy.* Cambridge: Cambridge UP, 1975.
[8] *Cf.* James Hillman. *The Dream and the Underworld*, New York: HarperCollins, 1979. This book is a fuller treatment of the Hades realm.
[9] *Cf.* James Hillman. "Alchemical Blue and the *Unio Mentalis,*" *Spring 54, 1993*, Woodstock, Spring Publications, 1993.

ALCHEMY OF THE BLUES

STEPHEN DIGGS

Are the color of one's skin, the color of one's land, and the color of one's soul connected? This is a dangerous question to ask in our time because the answers to such questions have been used in the past by people of light skin to degrade people of dark skin. To ask the question is to risk an answer that might be used again to degrade. Today our collective cultural ego has at last established that such degradation is wrong and its devastation must be ended. This is very good. Unfortunately, in the way of the ego, that collective has insisted that the remedy for the problem is to make the question wrong. We called this repression. As is often the case with the ego in its efforts to ease guilt and anxiety, the question is attacked instead of the problem, an action that can, and often does, inadvertently make the problem worse. Curiosity, in turn, may be a better remedy.

Like many white men and women who have been touched deeply by blues-based music, I have an intense curiosity about the "souls of black folk" and, likewise, the color of my own soul. Through the years my interest, nay, obsession with racial issues has led me to the difficult conviction that people with dark skin

---

Stephen Diggs works as a psychotherapist for the County of Plumas, California. He says he, "flails the blues on a Fender Stratocaster and an Ibenen 'Birdland.'"

have darker souls and people with light skins have lighter souls. The blues unflinchingly teaches this fact. The best and most famous white blues players, Stevie Ray Vaughan, Janis Joplin, Ry Cooder, Eric Clapton, can come close but never really achieve the dark soulfulness of the average black blues player let alone the greats like Howlin' Wolf, Charlie Parker, Bessie Smith. Is it cultural? Very likely. Is it genetic? Heaven forbid. Is it the color of the soul? Of course.

When the white supremacist asks the question about skin color and soul it is with the intent to claim the inferiority of dark-skinned people. Fortunately, we white blues players have a way to ask the question that is devoid of that intention. We white blues boys have turned the question on its head because we ask it with the goal of honoring the black soul and, ultimately, emulating it. The fact that we fail in our attempts to play the blues and so in emulating that soul leads to the conclusion that our souls in some way are not up to the task. They are . . . too white. So, I and other failed white blues players are probably the proper ones to ask the question because, if anything, it is we who feel degraded or, better said, humbled by it.

To answer this "racial" question I will pursue two directions of the movement of psyche in relation to the body. The first is the way in which projection and introjection color the soul from the outside moving in. The second is the way that archetypes of color poetically color the physical world from the inside moving out. Then, I will tell an alchemical tale about the way in which the blues has changed the color of the collective American soul and, in the end, Western culture consciousness itself.

Color From The Outside In

It is a given in Jungian psychology that light-skinned people project their "shadow" onto dark-skinned people and that this is the cause of most racial problems. Eric Neumann's *Depth Psychology and a New Ethic* (1990) is a classic example of this idea. It is a simple, direct, and most certainly accurate explanation of how souls are colored through projection. Dark-skinned people have "dark and dirty souls" because light-skinned people cannot face their split or repressed negative qualities and so imagine that they exist in dark-skinned people. The psychic effects and related behavior of these projections eventually color the souls of dark-skinned people, such as American slaves, who must somehow endure the outcome. The problem is compounded by the fact that the projection is unconscious leaving light skins in authentic belief of the inferiority of dark skins. Even Abraham Lincoln believed that Negroes were inferior.

I cannot argue with this explanation, but I am concerned with its limits. In his forward to Neumann's book, C.G. Jung does a beautiful job of pointing out that such a view, if expressed with moral intent, unavoidably forces a narrowing of vision. If projection is the cause of dark souls in dark people, one cannot openly consider that darkness phenomenologically without abandoning the only acceptable moral position. The projection explanation creates a trap similar to that of political correctness in our time. The question is not repressed entirely, but its answer is monotheistic and, once given, closed to further consideration. Jung makes it clear that while the "chief cause" of neurosis is moral conflict, moral answers are inadequate to solve them. Psychological openness is the best way to resolve moral dilemmas.

Hillman catapults the projection explanation into a different realm with his idea that "white casts its own white shadow" (1986, 38). The "shadow" is not black, it is any color in its shadow position. That white sees its shadow as black is a function of white's predilection toward splitting and oppositional thinking. Hillman's idea liberates the soul's color identity from the trap of anti-projection moralism by giving all manner of colored souls a full range of psychological qualities. The white conscious and the white unconscious exist in and of themselves without the need to claim black as either. We do not need to stop projecting our "blackness" on dark-skinned people, rather we "should" recognize our own white shadow. His move also implies that the conscious and unconscious of white are qualitatively different from the conscious and unconscious of black or green or whatever color.

Hillman effectively rocks the foundation of the projection explanation but he claims that light-skinned people became identified with the white soul only recently. This "whitening" occurred during the Age of Exploration with the identification of dark-skinned people with "blackness." I accept the accuracy of his view but suggest that it, too, is limited. I think that we must ask why whites began to think of themselves as white in the first place. Did their skin invite them to assume the archetypal position of white, or was white consciousness already there anyway, or both? Is it purely coincidence that it was white skinned people who exaggerated the qualities of white consciousness? Projection alone cannot answer these questions.

It is a maxim of object relations theory that the infant internalizes psychologically the breast upon which it nurses and this breast represents core positions of early identity. I want to point out the very obvious fact that the infant who nurses at a dark-skinned breast internalizes darkness and the infant who nurses at a light-skinned breast internalizes lightness. It is a substantial failing of object relations theory that it does not give color a place in psychological development. Archetypal psychology has learned through careful observation that color has priority over other archetypes. Color consciousness seems to exert a psychological primacy over other forms of consciousness.

I propose that the internalized breast of color creates a fundamental consciousness within the infant. Kandinsky (1977) suggests that there are two "main results" of looking at color, the first physical, the second psychic. The psychic effect produces a "corresponding spiritual vibration" with definite effects on consciousness depending on the color. Thus, our psychic and spiritual states of consciousness are affected, perhaps dominated by the colors we see and, I would say, with which we identify. If a person draws identity from his mother's breast, from his family, and from his community, that identity will unavoidably reflect, to some degree, the skin color of these people. While the person will undoubtedly have a variety of states of consciousness, each at times manifesting psychologically as particular colors, his sustained identity will be significantly and primarily influenced by the color of his people and the color of his own skin.

Part of physiognomy is the color of the face. Who I am, to some degree, is the color I am. Because my citadel of metaphors, my personal referent, my body has specific qualities, those qualities must shape the personal imaginal state that is my identity. One of those qualities is the color of my skin. When I share a collective identity with my closest associates the color we are shapes that shared identity. The colors of skin that surround us will be internalized by us and the soul we organize around those colors will reflect the archetypal qualities of those colors. And if color is psychologically primary, skin color identity may have primacy over other forms of identity, such as gender.

But here is the dilemma. There seem to be limits on the degree to which people can internalize a soul color that is different from their skin color. White Southern infants who nursed on the breast of a beloved "mammy" likely had darker souls than their Northern counterparts who had no exposure to the dark soul. But even so, a fundamental whiteness remains in that Southern baby. Even if I do everything possible to identify with blacks in order to introject that black soul so that I may play the blues, there is a persistent whiteness to me that can only give so much. My face, my physiognomy, is white and, so it seems, is my soul. Projection and introjection together are not enough to answer this racial question which implies that we must move beyond psychology for a definitive explanation.

The Poetics of Matter

David Miller (1994) proposes that where psychology stops poetry must take over for knowing to continue. He invokes Lacan who says, "I am not a poet but a poem, a poem that is being written, even if it looks like a subject." While I believe this idea opens the door for an answer to our question, it also exposes a persistent problem with post-modernism that must be overcome in order to proceed. That problem: Where is the body? Where is the object? Where is matter? Hamilton asserts that "with the post-modern necessity to abandon the heroic fantasy of positivistic science, we have become lost in a universe of refraction and indeterminacy in which it has become sacrilege to attribute a quality or value to anything without being accused of Cartesian dualism" (1994). This leads unavoidably, says Hamilton, to a domination of the subjective. Paradoxically, deconstruction of the subject has led to subjectivism. To "overcome" Cartesian dualism is a reactionary move that merely replaces the obsession with objectivity with an obsession for subjectivity. As the "subject" is being deconstructed by post-modernism, subjectivism is taking over because the "object" disappears without its Cartesian opposite.

Modern Cartesian consciousness claimed separation of mind and body but in fact practiced mind/body unity. Because the only valid image was an exact "objective" replication of the referent a fascist but clearly congruent state of mind/body unity resulted. Post-modernism claims mind/body unity but practices a separation between mind and body through Hamilton's paradox. Cartesian mind/body dualism must be rejected in favor of theoretical unity, but in doing so we find that it is only in dualism that we experience phenomenologically the congruence of mind and body predicted by the theoretical unity. Paradoxically, qualities must be assigned through dualism for unity to occur. To find the congruency between mind and body, begin by splitting them.

Certainly I leave myself open to the charge of dualism by attributing the quality of blackness to dark-skinned people and the quality of whiteness to light-skinned people. And, in fact, I am proposing a dualism, a subject/object split. But, I am asking that the split come out of poetics, not literal science. The way out of the subject/subjectivism paradox is to include Lacan's body, his matter, as part of the poem. His matter is the objective part of his poem. Our acceptance of literal science and our emphasis on the primacy of image has convinced us that objective matter belongs to science and objective psyche to us. I propose that objective matter does belong to us but poetically, not literally. Deconstruction of the subject need not result in the loss of the object if we hold fast to the idea that objective matter is a poetic reality as well as a scientific one and that the aesthetic imperatives of poetry are as powerful and relevant to objective matter as the natural laws of science.

Or perhaps it is this. If psyche is the object, then matter becomes the subject. And if there is no subject, only a poem being written, then the body becomes the poem. The objective psyche in its archetypal forms writes poems that are bodies.

I remember the dead body of my friend and first clinical supervisor, Ken, lying in a casket. It was clearly not him. He was dead and gone though I could feel his spirit nearby. Yet as I looked, it was clear that his body was the most perfect expression of who he was psychologically. His body evoked his psychic essence so precisely that I had the feeling that he would sit up at any moment and laugh. His nearby spirit evoked no such essential feeling. The matter that was his body was part of the poem that was Ken. Psyche and spirit wrote him not only as an individual personality poem, but also as matter that was that poem in the physical world.

The body is not only a citadel of metaphors that feeds the psyche, it is also an objective citadel that best expresses the psyche. If Ken's personal body is the best expression of his personal psyche, then could it be possible that our collective bodies are likewise the best expression of our collective psyche. The best place to look to know the nature of our collective psyches may not be our myths, it may be our bodies. To the degree that our collective psyches are archetypally formulated so also are our bodies archetypal poetic expressions. The bodies of white skin people are poetic expressions of the archetype of white. And if the archetype of white does indeed create white skin people, it does so from within their collective soul so that their racial character must also reflect that whiteness. The poem of whiteness is both my skin and my soul.

Literal science says that my skin is light because my ancestors came from a place with long winters, lots of clouds, and little sunlight, therefore, they did not need much skin pigment, melanin, to avoid sunburn and in fact got more of the sun's benefit because of its lack. Literal science says Langston Hughes had dark skin because his ancestors came from a place with near constant sun and so developed large amounts of melanin for protection as an adaptation. Langston Hughes himself says:

> I am a Negro
> Black as the night is black,
> Black like the depths of my Africa.
> (1959)

It is unclear whether the "I" he is referring to is his skin or his soul, but one gets the feeling that he is not separating them. His skin and his soul are merely different reflections of the same identity. His poem suggests that his dark identity is an expression, a metaphor, of the dark depths of Africa. His color identity is an exposition of the soul of his land. Recall Jung in Africa sensing that "a darkness altogether different from natural night broods over the land" (298). Recall Joseph Conrad's *Heart of Darkness*. Are these racist stereotypes or accurate perceptions? Hughes, certainly no Uncle Tom, seems entirely comfortable with the idea that these are accurate perceptions. Can it be that psyche, spirit, soul made African people dark-skinned and dark-souled as a poetic act that metaphorically matched the nature of their land? Are black skin and black soul a rhyme?

We might call it an "enduring synchronicity." As such it is an acausal effect of psyche on matter that lasts beyond the moment. This is not a theophany nor an epiphany nor a premonitory dream nor the loud report of a bookcase, but psyche making lasting metaphors in the physical world. A scientific, literal explanation must by definition be causal. At the opposite pole to science is poetry and the acausal perspective. Let us take this perspective, retain the separation of psyche and matter, but throw out causality in favor of poetry. In doing so we might be able to abduct matter back from the literal, for it is in matter that psyche and spirit write their poems. Matter exists separately to contribute forms for *imagos* to psyche and to manifest poems for psyche. Psyche exists separately to experience imaginally the forms of matter and to shape matter according to its rich imaginal variations.

This view forces the question, how could people with dark skin not have darker souls and how could people with light skin not have lighter souls? The two must certainly reflect each other. Of course we should not get literal about this. The shunning of Cartesian dualism in favor of a poetic dualism can result in its own literalism. Here, psyche and matter always must have a congruence that leaves no room for the freedom psyche needs to make objective poems that vary according to the mood of the poet. To guard against this literalism we should leave substantial room for the diversity of the poet's impulses and its acausal nature.

Consider the variation of the individual color constitution of the soul. Perhaps the poet colors each person a unique and individual mix of the humors—black, rose, green, and yellow—and this mix is as stable as a racial color constitution. This fundamental color orientation and identity of the individual personality would, in combination with the racial identity, shape the physical body in a poetic fashion. As a result, I would expect that a phlegmatic Negro person would be of a different sort than a phlegmatic Asian person. The poet mixes colors in all fashions; yellow on a white background, green on a black background, and so on.

Or, compare these poems to the transsexual. Her psyche is clearly not in congruence with her matter. She is a woman trapped in the body of a man. Could there also be those who are not in congruence with their skin tone? We could invent disorders of racial identity. Slang knows these conditions. The "Oreo" is black on the outside and white on the inside. Is there such a thing as a black man trapped in the body of a white man? Most of us white blues failures would say yes. On the street we are called "wiggers." These exceptions help the case for a poetics of matter, for in these situations mind and body are clearly split and psyche dominates identity in spite of the literal matter of the body. The psyche goes to great extremes to require the body to become the object of the poem. For the transsexual this might mean hormone therapy, cosmetic extremes, and even surgery to remove the matter that is incongruent to the poem. For the white blues player it can mean hours and years of frustration and failure, abandoning a successful career in the white business world, little or no money, no family life, addiction. Anything to play the blues.

Like other psychological qualities in the personality, perhaps there are color features in each individual that are relatively stable and unchanging and color features that have great latitude for variation, pathology, and creativity. The racial and humor color identities may be relatively fixed while the emotional and alchemical color identities ebb and flow and transform. I suggest that these color dynamics can be used to construct personal and cultural narratives that tell psychological stories in terms of the ways in which the stable and mutable states of color consciousness interact. It is to such a narrative that I have turned to make sense of my obsession with race and the blues.

Like many white people who have an unfathomable passion for African-American music my color narrative is one in which black and white have played a central role. In order to play the music I love, I have tried for many years to be darker. I have succeeded a little and failed often, for I am Caucasian, white like the snow is white, white like the heights of Europe. My personal color narrative has revealed much to me about the basic nature of my soul and the fixed color identities that allow me to go only so far in the deeper darkening of my soul. But what it seems unable to reveal is the reason that I, and so many other whites like me, keep coming back to the blues in spite of the persistent experience of failure. To see through this insanity I was forced to try and tell the story of the larger cultural color narrative that encases the blues. What I found is a stunning tale of race relations and the transformation of the Western mind.

An Alchemical Tale

I propose that there are two histories of America: one is conscious and economic, the other unconscious and alchemical. Nowhere is this experienced more than in race. Africans were stolen into American slavery to satisfy the conscious economic desire to create wealth but also to satisfy the unconscious alchemical desire for psychological transformation. They were both cheap labor and "the nigredo." And while the unconscious white fantasy ostensibly had a missionary zeal toward saving the "blacks" from their nigredo hell, the other side of the fantasy, the unconscious of the unconscious, was bent on saving the Western soul from its psychotic flight from the body. Only the nigredo can "break into bits" the singular vision and dissociative defenses of the supreme white mind (Hillman, 1986). The essential literalism of that mind required that Africans be that nigredo. If the American Dream is economic, the American Nightmare is alchemical.

Jamestown, Virginia, 1619. Slavery is that nightmare, or at least its most visible representation. Many writers have pointed out that the true treachery of American slavery was not so much slavery itself but the attitudes that surrounded it (*e.g.,* Jones, 1963; Du Bois, 1994; Williams, 1991). Historically, throughout the world, slavery has taken many forms of degradation. There were forms of European and African slavery in which a slave had substantial liberty, could make money, have a family, and even purchase freedom. In these forms the slave was considered a person, and so it was for Africans in early American slavery. In early Virginia, African slaves had the legal status of indentured servants and their baptism was a bar against enslavement. But the attitudes toward African slaves in America followed a progressive deterioration underpinned by the progression of the dissociative flight of the white mind. In 1661, the Virginia Assembly passed a law differentiating African slaves from white indentured servants, making the Africans slaves for life. Within 100 years the deterioration was complete, typified by a Maryland law which put African and African-American slaves in the same category as "working beasts, animals of any kind, stock, furniture, plate, books, and so forth" (Foster, 37).

Clearly this attitude was a psychological defense of rationalization to justify the economic benefit of lifetime slavery. But it was more than that as well. The quality of the defense betrays the psychotic state of dissociation that, in this case, is at minimum delusional and possibly even a mass hallucination. How can one look at a *homo sapiens* and not see a *homo sapiens*, but instead see a working beast or a piece of furniture? The white unconscious could not bear to identify with the evil it was doing and so called upon defenses that were consistent with its dissociative pathology to avoid this awareness. But we must ask, what does the symptom want?

Seeing humans as things suggests a desire of the white mind to be returned to the status of a human "thing among things" (Hillman, 1986, 54). It is a projected wish to get out from behind the walls of the white mind and return to the materiality of the world. It is a wish to be brought down. The higher up the white mind went, the lower down it had to push the image of its shadow, the African slaves. This temporarily maintained its defensive homeostasis, but in the long run this breathless repression inevitably created a powerful nigredo poised to break the white mind to bits.

North and South. The white mind in colonial America naturally did what comes natural to it; it split in order to create oppositionalisms. The two splits of significance for this tale are the North/South split and the house/field split. North and South during the Age of Exploration were imagined by the Western mind in a way that Africa was black hell and Europe was white heaven. I suggest that pristine America was unconsciously imagined to be *prima materia* in a sterile hermetic vessel into which the North/South opposition could be introjected. If the white mind was unconsciously stealing slaves to be the nigredo that would break it to bits, then it was inevitable that the playing out of this alchemy would be done in terms of the central metaphor of the split, North and South. Importantly, perhaps necessarily, the vertical geographic span of America provided it with adequate climatic difference to underpin the imagining.

The traditional split of North as white and South as black was greatly, and necessarily, complicated in America with the latitudinal political splitting of the land by the white mind at the Mason-Dixon line. This act resulted in the splitting of the white mind itself. Here, now, were two kinds of white mind, one North and one South; one cool and one hot. This development would prove to be essential for the alchemy because it forced the white mind to turn its oppositionalism in on itself, rather than keeping it focused on the Africans. While this turn inward was carried out in relationship to the nigredo as represented by the Africans, it was primarily narcissistic, for now the white mind was projecting onto itself.

The tension between the northern industrial liberal and the southern agricultural conservative is the central theme of American politics. The tragi-comic truth, however, is that both sides are actually the same white mind, fundamentally identical, merely having reached different conclusions about what it means to be supreme. The southern conservative concluded that supremacy meant keeping the nigredo repressed while the northern liberal concluded that supremacy meant lifting the nigredo up to the light. What neither could imagine (and what many still cannot) was that the nigredo was brought here to bring down the white mind in whatever form of supremacy it is in.

This paper owes much to LeRoi Jones and his classic work *The Blues People* (1963). In his book Jones points out that there were two kinds of slaves in America, house slaves and field slaves. The house slaves were considered superior to the field slaves by virtue of their exposure to whites within the house. As a result they were at odds with the field slaves whom they felt to be primitive and uncouth. The house slaves' primary adaptation was identification with the aggressor. House slaves went on to become the "black middle class" through their use of craft, trade, and technical skill developed in and around the house. The field slaves, who did only manual agricultural labor, went on to become the "black underclass." The masterful splitting of the white mind is evidenced in the persistence of the tension between these two groups in post-slavery times, up to the present.

Jones calls house slaves "white Negroes." Here is the beginning of the alchemy. The African slave is brought into the house of the white master, sealed in that hermetic vessel, and changed through association with that master into a "white Negro" or, as we say in alchemy, the albedo. The white mind changed the nigredo into albedo through the transformation of the house slave. Now, if the alchemy works both ways as Hillman (1986) claims, we would expect the white master also to be changed into the albedo by the house slave. But this did not happen. In fact, the master found his sense of supremacy reinforced by his ability to transform the nigredo. This reveals the alchemical power of the split, for it is the field slave, not the house slave, who eventually takes the white mind to the albedo by inventing and disseminating the blues. It will take the lowest of the low to bring down the soaring white mind.

Colonial America ended, of course, with the Revolutionary War. The conscious economic reasons for the war are quite apparent, those who lived here did not want to share the wealth of the continent with Europe. But underneath this obvious rationale, alchemy was at work. The war, along with isolationism and the Monroe Doctrine, can be viewed as a sealing of the vessel so that the alchemy of the white mind could begin. The doctrine of liberty, which is part and parcel of the economic fantasy, was important to the alchemy as a symptomatic opening into the denials of the white mind, for eventually the absurdity of speaking of liberty in a nation of legalized slavery would begin to open the door for the release of the nigredo into white society.

The Civil War. By splitting itself between North and South the white mind became stuck in an unsolvable paradox of the supremacy of white. "How can I repress my inferiors and simultaneously display my goodness by helping them to be like me?" The unsolvability of the split assured that the single vision of the white mind would grow ever more fragile, making eventual breakdown into nigredo possible. This fragility created tremendous internal tension as the two halves battled each other to determine which form of supremacy would reign supreme. The tension created the heat that the alchemy required, the culmination of which was the nigredo we call the Civil War.

The excess, the intensity, the hatred, the tenacity, the passion, the insanity of the war suggest, as we all know, that mere economics were not at the bottom of this struggle. At the bottom was the process that had been pushing the white mind's penchant for oppositionalism to unbelievable extremes during the Piscian aion: the archetypal motif of the hostile brothers. But no longer was the white mind at odds with its anti-Christian black "brother." As the Western mind continued its dissociative flight it got so far out of touch with everyone and everything that it was forced to implode and play out its oppositionalism with the only one left with whom it remained in contact, itself. White cast its own white shadow and projected onto itself: North on South and South on North.

If we employ a metaphor of therapist and patient, the Civil War might be imagined as the critical therapeutic impasse in which the patient, as Southern conservative, is in intense resistance within the transference and is battling the therapist, as Northern liberal, who is attempting "bring up" the repressed complex, or African-American slave. The Emancipation Proclamation releases the shadow, the nigredo, and the patient must admit the defeat of his ego which has failed to keep the complex subservient. This brings on a depression or blue period. The "enlightened" white mind of the therapist has won over the "repressive" white mind of the patient's ego. The therapist hopes that the shadow, now free, will be "integrated" by the patient who no longer will have the need to project his unconscious hatred and aggression. The therapist himself, however, wants to remain in his detached place, unchanged and unaffected by that shadow.

North and South were not fundamentally different, they were merely different faces of supreme white. The fact that the symbology of the struggle crystallized around the issue of slavery suggests that African-Americans had moved into the role of nigredo as change agent of the white mind, not the substance to be changed by it. Indeed, the war over slavery did smash to bits the singular vision of the American white mind. But this breakdown alone was not enough to bring about a true transformation of that mind.

The Birth of the Blues. The implosion of the white mind upon itself in the Civil War and the resultant release of African-Americans into the culture at large through emancipation allowed the alchemical transformation of the white mind by the nigredo to move to its next stage: blue consciousness. Immediately after the war and during Reconstruction, African-Americans began creating the fundamental agent of white mind change, the blues.

In "Alchemical Blue and the *Unio Mentalis*," Hillman (1993) says that in the movement toward the albedo a series of other colors can arise:

> ...notably darker blues, the blues of bruises, sobriety, puritan self-examination; the blues of slow jazz...The blue transit between black and white is like that sadness which emerges from despair as it proceeds towards reflection...(It) can also show as blue movies, blue language...Blue protects white from innocence...The transit from black to white via blue implies blue always brings black with it... It is the element of depression, that raises deep doubts and high principals, wanting to settle things fundamentally and get them right in order to clarify them. (132) The *unio mentalis* implies a divine drunkenness... Dionysos... sees with the blue eye and to see him our eye must be colored the same way (141-142).

Now I will take a bold and probably foolish step. I will try to explain why the blues are called the blues. To my knowledge, no one has ever seriously attempted or been successful at such an explanation. The obvious reason for this is that no one before now has explored the blues archetypally. But it is more than that. In the artistic world of the blues an attempt such as this would be condemned as unnecessary, absurd, and even dangerous to the vitality of the music. This step might be akin to an archeologist digging up ancestor graves for "scientific purposes." Because of my long association with the blues I am acutely aware of the arrogance of what I am attempting and I want to acknowledge that aloud out of respect for the blues. But perhaps the real arrogance is how serious I am about taking the step. Most blues people would laugh to think that a white psychologist was explaining the blues.

The blues are called the "blues" because they satisfy the archetypal requirements and the specific cultural and historical necessities to function as the manifest blue or *unio mentalis* of the unconscious alchemy of race in America. The blues effects change in African-Americans and European-Americans as they have come to hold the psychology of black and white in a literalized enactment of the alchemical nightmare of the dissociative Western mind in its move toward a union of opposites, or albedo, at the end of our age. That they are called the "blues" confirms my proposal of an unconscious alchemy, for what else could have produced this name but a cultural archetypal process that identified people by color and then cast them together in a "melting-pot."

During Reconstruction many former house slaves went on to apply their trades in the open labor market, though often with poor success as angry backlash left them chronically unemployed. But former field slaves had it even worse. With little or nothing to offer for employment the government gave them "forty acres and a mule" and instructed them to farm. Psychologically this action is based in the Western fantasy of individuality. In Africa and on the plantation the life of field slaves had been tribal and communal. The government could have given them large communal plots to farm together but instead they were given single family dwellings and asked to be individuals. It was these people who first created the blues. Says Jones:

> African songs dealt, as did the songs of a great many of the preliterate or classical civilizations, with the exploits of the social unit,

usually the tribe...The insistence of the blues verse on the life of the individual and his individual trials and successes on earth is a manifestation of the whole Western concept of man's life, and it is a development that could only be found in an American black man's music (66).

The original blues was a personal solo music concerning the individual musician who was making it. As such, it was based on the "I," self, or ego of the West as it came to be introjected into the rural unskilled African-American. In stealing Africans, Europeans, who were lost in their fantasy of individual consciousness, were stealing a communal, tribal, oral tradition. Slaves practiced this tradition when working together in the fields singing work songs. Sitting alone on their forty acres those work songs turned into the blues. For the first time field slaves had the leisure and space necessary to turn their dark despair into blue sadness on their way toward reflection.

As African consciousness passed through the blues and on toward the albedo, its primary change was the development of the Western fantasy of the individual. This individuality had already been introjected into house slaves but they were required to reject communal consciousness in order to receive it. Within the blues musicians that "I" or ego became integrated with the older forms of oral tradition that the field slaves had continued to carry in their collective soul. Here is the beginning of the albedo that is the union of the opposites, "I" and "we."

The blues of these musicians reflects Hillman's images of blue as the "*unio mentalis*" of alchemy, containing Truth, depression, and libido. Says James Cone (99, 102), "Implied in the blues is a stubborn refusal to go beyond the existential problem and substitute otherworldly answers...(T)o understand them it is necessary to view the blues as a state of mind in relation to the Truth of black experience." And what is that truth? "The blues are an artistic rebellion against the humiliating deadness of western culture."

The blues transformed European-American consciousness in the same way it transformed African-American consciousness; through an albedo in which western individual consciousness melded with tribal orality. At every turn, the blues smashed down the walls of isolation of the white individual mind. But it also did much more than this. It is most likely that the alchemical transformation of African consciousness was fateful but not necessary, while the transformation of the white mind was fateful and necessary. Contained in the blues is a stubborn refusal to go beyond the truth that the dissociative splitting, isolation, and humiliating deadness of the western mind were reeking havoc on the world. Because of this extreme pathology, transformation of the white mind was not optional. Through the racial alchemy of America the white mind was to be taken to the albedo via blue and in that way disarmed of its supremacist arsenal. The blue that would do it would have to be able to break down the fascism of soulless scientific materialism by doing therapy on its language and consciousness, and by seducing it down from its dissociative heights. The blues was just such a force accomplishing its therapy and seduction with depression, rhythm, intoxication, and libido.

I have built a cultural narrative about the transformation of Western consciousness through African-American music by focusing on color and alchemy. Twelve years ago, in *Shadow Dancing in the USA* (1985), Michael Ventura arrived at many of the conclusions I have reached here by constructing a historical narrative about jazz and rock 'n' roll that focused on a return to the body through the *loa* or spirit possession of the musician and listener/dancer. Both Ventura and Julio Finn (1986) show that bluesmen are the secular carriers of the Hoodoo or Voodoo religion which is a hybrid of traditional West African religions and Christianity. As such, bluesmen and women tend to spirit and psyche in a manner handed down from Africa to Hoodoo; spirit possession. Where the Northern soul, from shaman to Christian priest, operates dissociatively, leaving the body to travel the spirit world, the African priest, the Hoodoo conjurer, and the bluesmen ask the *loa* to enter bodies and possess them. It is through this possession that the *loa* is known and expressed. It is said that B.B. King needs two hours to exit the possession trance of his performances. Return to the body, says the blues. Says Ventura:

> The history of America is, as much as anything, the history of the American body as it sought to unite with its spirit, with its consciousness, to heal itself and to stand against the enormous forces that work to destroy a Westerner's relationship to his, or her, own flesh. This music, largely unaware of itself, carried forward through the momentum of deeply rooted instinct; contradicting itself in many places; perverting its own purposes in many instances; sinking many times under the weight of its own intensity into the nether world of hate and confusion and bad trips; and trivializing its own meanings at many a crucial turn; this music, yet trusted, rushes through every area of this country's life in aural "great awakening" all its own, to quicken the body and excite the spirit and, quite literally, to awaken the dead. (159)

Blues lyrics have tremendous breadth, within which are two core streams, depression and libido. The depressive quality of the blues is the most recognizable to the majority of people, an example of which is the lament for being "done wrong" by a lover. But the blues is also highly sexual and at times exuberant. There are many "happy" blues about good time fun, including the joys of food and dance. The blues is about the passions of the flesh. Where the pathological Western mind tended to create dirty movies out of this blue, blacks turned these libidinous hurricanes into the huge body of art called the blues. In the hands of dissociative consciousness blue veers toward pornography; in the hands of rhythmic consciousness toward art.

Depression and passion in the blues finds a strong association with Dionysos' blueness as "somber madness" and instinctual sexuality. In *Stomping the Blues* (1976), Albert Murray says that in the "dance hall as temple" the "fundamental function of the blues musician (also known as the jazz musician)...is not only to drive away the blues and hold them at bay at least for the time being, but also to evoke an ambiance of Dionysian revelry in the process" (17). And so, the blues, commonly known as the "Devils music" in all of its myriad forms (jazz, rock'n'roll, rap, etc.) is most at home in our modern temples to Dionysos: juke joints, night clubs, bars, whorehouses, and "blue light" districts.

It is fascinating to note that in addition to the lyric content of the blues, its music and performance practices also worked to transform the dissociative consciousness. Harmonically, the blues is based on the tritone interval (*e.g.,* F/B) which is considered the most dissonant of all intervals and thus full of tension. In Renaissance times this interval was known as the "*Diabolus en musica*" (Lee, 17) and for a time its use in performance was actually illegal. It was eventually returned to Western harmony but only in the tension of the dominant chord as it resolved into the purity, consonance and "salvation" of the tonic chord. In the blues, almost every chord contains the tritone, even the tonic. The problem of union of the opposites is managed in the blues by permeating the music with the tension of the tritone. The Christian Devil is everywhere, the dream of salvation nowhere.

The musical feature most idiosyncratic to the blues is the flattening of certain notes. It is this that gives the blues its moanful expression. The performer either starts on the note and falls off the pitch or starts below it and with a pregnant weariness fails to reach the pitch. In a most elegant synchronicity the scale numbers that are pulled down happen to be those great Christian numbers, three and seven. These scaled pitches, three (E in C major) and seven (B in C major), are known as leading tones and are the fundamentals of Western music's greatest accomplishment, vertical harmony. As leading tones, their movement is upward, leaving the earth, on towards transcendence. Their stylistic dominance began, not surprisingly, in the Baroque period when the dissociative process of the white mind was escalating during the Age of Exploration. The blues pulls on that upwardness, as if to say, come back to earth.

By now I hope you have become quite annoyed with the inconsistent conjugation of the verbs following the word blues in this paper. Like the practice in blues-based cultures, I decide whether to make the verb plural or singular intuitively, in the moment of writing. Sometimes the blues *is* and sometimes the blues *are*. From its inception the blues managed with ease the problem of the one and the many, the "I" and the "we." Rather than confront this potential oppositionalism, either singular or plural, the blues simply made itself both singular and plural. This is not the only way everyday speech is expressively altered by the blues.

In performance, but also in the daily language of blues-based cultures, the distinctions between utterances, rhythm, and meaning are often blurred and the ambiguities between them accentuated. Words may be slurred so that meaning can only be accessed through a reading of emotional and rhythmic context. Or a word may be stated clearly but the meaning known only through the quality of expression. For example, the word "bad" covers a huge area of meaning from bad to good to virile to decrepit to many a subtle mixture of several valances. Discerning the meaning of bad on the printed page is very difficult because the significance of this word in blues culture is to be found in the moment from within oral consciousness. This linguistic style reflects the fundamental way in which African speech and music are different from European languages and music in modernity. Says Ernest Borneman:

> While the whole European tradition strives for regularity—of pitch, of time and vibrato—the African tradition strives precisely for the negation of these elements. In language, the African tradition aims at circumlocution rather than at exact definition. The direct statement is considered crude and unimaginative; the veiling of all contents in ever-changing paraphrases is considered the criterion of intelligence and personality. In music, the same tendency toward obliquity and ellipsis is noticeable: no note is attacked straight; the voice or instrument always approaches it from above or below, plays around the implied pitch without ever remaining any length of time, and departs from it without ever having committed itself to a single meaning...The timing and accentuation, finally, are not stated, but implied or suggested. The denying or withholding of all signposts. (cited in Jones, 31)

In the simpler words of the blues tradition, "It ain't what you say, it's how you say it." Long before post-modernism, the blues loved to deny the referent. While both are able and willing to unhinge the scientific materialist fantasy of objectivity through that denial, the ultimate effect from within African-American consciousness is much different than the effect of post-modern denial. That words refer only to themselves is a problem only when they are locked up by themselves behind the walls of white oppositional consciousness. If the subject is words and the subject is opposed to the object, then words are opposed to objects. Post-modernism is denial of the referent from within oppositional consciousness, the result of which is Hamilton's paradox of subjectivism.

African linguistic/musical consciousness, and thus the blues, does not ask words to refer but neither does it isolate them as opposed to the referent. As Duke Ellington said, "You have to find a way to say it without really saying it." African consciousness asks words to live among things and ideas not to know them but rather to serve as the substance for a process that creates relationships between them so that in those relationships knowing may occur. By allowing a person to live in relationship with things rather than in opposition to them the body is affirmed, rather than lost, as in post-modernism. The body is allowed to be a thing among things. This is language as communal consciousness, not oppositional consciousness. Stunningly, blues consciousness as albedo extends psyche even further than African consciousness alone. In the blues, the union of communal and individual consciousness allows the individual to be affirmed *without* the oppositionalism of subject and object. The individual speaks of himself, but with a language that services a commune of things and ideas of which he is one.

Unio mentalis consciousness also allows the blues to do something different with the denial of the referent as it relates to the truth. Where the post-modern mind has created an oppositionalism between the semiotic process of signification and the archetype of the truth, the blues, in its functional role as the *unio mentalis*, is able to unite them. In the blues, the veiling and denial are not at odds with the truth, they are ways to reveal it. The blues is able to break down the tyranny of scientific objectivism without disavowing what is essential.

The blues that developed in post-Reconstruction America was a collective psychology that expressed the union of Western individual literate consciousness with African tribal orality. As such it was poised to change the American descendants of Africa and Europe in somewhat equal measure. To the Africans it would bring the psychology of individuality. To the Europeans it would bring depression and passions of the flesh as a way to return to materiality and a sense of communality. It would do so by manifesting itself as a language capable of breaking down the scientific literary consciousness that was holding the West captive. This in turn would create a space for a new white and a new black to appear; the albedo.

19th Century Vienna. In Vienna they like to sit and listen. Vienna is the site where Beethoven, completing the task begun by Classicists, made non-participatory music the undisputed dictator of Western music. In Renaissance times, dance and music were inseparable and religious music was always part of a participatory Mass. But dance and religion as a focus for composition began to fade with the Baroque and were fully subservient as the Classical period came to an end. In the Romantic period music was all but synonymous with sitting and listening. Beethoven's Third Symphony is considered a pivotal piece in this transition because sitting and listening to music was based on the "extra-musical thought" that it should be an individualistic personal confession (Jacobson, 10) and the Third Symphony was one of the first to embody this quality. As a music instructor once told me, Mozart is the last composer you can listen to without hearing an ego trip. With Mozart it was the voice of the community, with Beethoven the voice of the individual. Should we be surprised the Third Symphony is called the "Eroica"?

Three blocks away from the site where Beethoven wrote the Third Symphony in Vienna, Freud wrote *The Interpretation of Dreams,* the inspiration for the work coming from sitting and listening to the personal confessions of his Viennese patients. The consciousness that made the music is somehow connected to the consciousness that invented psychoanalysis.

The body, the feminine, darkness, depression, and the passions of the flesh were all given great prominence by early depth psychologists, but because these men and women were locked into the mind-set of their cultural and historical moment, they were unable to affirm on its own terms the unconscious they found so fascinating. Instead, they determined, perhaps unavoidably, that the great underbelly of the white mind needed a remedy and that remedy should be more white mind. Where the id was, the ego shall be. Because it was grounded in the dissociative symptomatic consciousness of the white mind, their method was doomed to perpetuate the very fault it would resolve. Sitting and listening to the individual was the problem; it could not also be the answer. These darker elements of body and psyche wanted to be promoted by their own Dionysian language, not rehabilitated by the rational language of the white mind. They wanted to be embodied, not replaced.

If depth psychology failed to transform the white mind because it was that white mind, the blues succeeded greatly in changing the white mind precisely because it was something else.

The Blues Revolution. The blues revolution is a psycho-cultural process in which the blues unites with an African-American dance-rhythm music and a particular style of European-American music to create a new form of music. At first, only African-Americans participate in the new form but soon European-Americans are attracted to the way in which the depression, sensuality, ambiguity, and dance-rhythm provided by the African elements have breathed a new life into the European musical form. As Europeans begin to participate in the music, it enters into the mainstream culture and transforms the white mind by bringing it back down to earth through the change of consciousness brought about by the music and the new communal Dionysian culture that has organized around it. The new music absorbs and becomes central to the cutting-edge technology of its time which adds to its potency and provides resilience to the powerful resistances of the dominant white culture. Though they are powerful, these resistances prove to be futile since this return, this alchemy, is the symptomatic creation of the white mind culture itself.

The blues revolution is Dionysos inciting the instinctual maenads to pull Pentheus from the treetop back down to earth and then tear his detached vision to bits in a dreadful nigredo. It is Huck and Jim traveling down the Mississippi together to escape the abuses of the white patriarchy and find some sense of truth. These images are congruent with the strong association between blacks, women, and youth within the revolution. In the Western imagination, both women and blacks are assigned the qualities of instinct, body, and primitiveness and both carry the repressed and projected qualities of that imagination in modernity. In the revolution, the liberation from this white repression is brought about by a soulful conspiracy between blacks, women, and youth whose central battles and political gains run parallel to each other.

The blues revolution manifests itself in a series of cycles, roughly forty years in length. As twentieth-century American mythology is organized around decades, I will describe these cycles in terms of four distinctly identifiable and repeating decades. In the first decade (1900, 1940, 1980), white conservatism rises and produces a backlash against gains by blacks. Ghettoed again, blacks create a new form of dance-oriented blues. In the second decade (1910, 1950, 1990) blacks respond politically by creating and beginning to exercise new agendas to meet the backlash. Some whites take interest in the new music and begin to play it. In the third decade (1920, 1960) a bacchanalia occurs. The new dance music triggers a blues-based return to the passions of the flesh. Intoxication and fornication surge as youth and women join blacks in a rejection of white patriarchal values. The fourth decade (1930, 1970) is one of collapse following the bacchanalia. Absorbing the change it went through, the white mind recovers from depression, addiction, and the assorted pains incurred during its violent return to materiality.

Cycle One: The Jazz Revolution. The first wave of the blues revolution began with the creation of jazz around the turn of the century (Jones, 1963; Foster, 1953; Ogren, 1989). White backlash against the gains of blacks during Reconstruction resulted in Jim Crow laws and a renewed imposition of segregation that drove Creoles, who had formerly enjoyed much freedom in French dominated Louisiana, back into ghettos. Many of the Creoles were skilled with European instruments used in town bands at the time. They joined these instruments with the drumming popular on Congo Square in New Orleans and the Delta blues of the field slaves with whom they now shared the ghetto, and jazz was born. In the first decade of the revolution, 1900, the great sounds of Buddy Bolden and King Oliver and Jelly Roll Morton were shocking and seductive to the Victorian, white mind.

In her book, *The Jazz Revolution*, Kathy Ogren (1989) tracks the intense controversy over jazz at the turn of the century. She says that Americans shared a common perception that "jazz had transforming qualities that could last beyond the time of the song and the space of the cabaret act. For many Americans, to argue about jazz was to argue about the nature of change itself." Those fearful of it said it was primal, uncivilized, and demolished moral constraint, while "jazz lovers hailed [it] as an antidote for repressive industrial society" (7). The qualities of jazz that made it so controversial were those fundamental to oral consciousness: it is felt bodily and it is participatory. Over and over this music is defined by people of this time as a "language" that requires participation and moves the body. These features are present throughout the music but exemplified by the "call and response" fundamental to African music and the inseparability of dance and song.

In the second decade blacks began political organization with the creation of the N.A.A.C.P. and the Urban League. The field slave/house slave tension was felt in attitudes toward assimilation epitomized by the differing positions of W. E. B. Du Bois, who pushed for assimilation, and Booker T. Washington, who favored building African-American power from within their own community (Du Bois, 1994; George, 1988). Women likewise were involved in strong political assertion with the suffrage movement.

Whites began to be drawn to jazz. The sweet and syrupy sounds of the "King of Jazz," Paul Whiteman (what a lovely synchronicity that name is!), represented the banal co-opting of the music, while Bix Beiderbecke created some of the first soulful white jazz.

In 1920 the "Jazz Age" bacchanalia exploded. A "lost generation" of youth flew with great abandon into the passions of the flesh, riding upon the sounds of jazz which dominated the new technology of phonography. The chastity and sobriety of women was compromised everywhere as their bodies awakened under the tutorial of the Charleston—which Jones identifies as an Ashanti ancestor dance (1963, 17). Church and civic leaders were aghast. Fueled by tobacco and alcohol, protected by the new technology of contraception, and led by the never-before-heard sounds of Louis Armstrong, these maenadic flappers went into head-on battle with Pentheus and his obsession with control.

"Inspired by Sigmund Freud [and those who tracked the repression presumed to be endemic to Western civilization], twenties artists and intellectuals invested primitive culture with 'uncivilizing' virtues...Experiencing jazz could release and rejuvenate buried emotions or instincts" (Ogren, 146). Freud wanted the ego to replace the id; jazz wanted the id set free. And so it was in the first bacchanalia.

The fourth decade, 1930, contained the tragedy that always follows a bacchanalia. The nature of that tragedy supports my supposition of two American histories. The smashing to bits of the singular vision of the white mind in the nigredo of the twenties resulted in the delivery of the blues to the conscious economic fantasy which the nation experienced as the "Great Depression." Yes, the story of the Depression can be told in economic language, but it can also be told as a color narrative. In the latter telling, the unconscious alchemy of the blues pulled the body of the white economic fantasy, the corporation, to its knees.

Cycle Two: The Rock 'n' Roll Revolution. In the 1940's blacks made many social and economic gains due to World War II. These came both from within the military and through industries supporting the military. This resulted in a backlash by white conservatives followed by a bitterness among blacks who saw their gains attacked. In this decade a new music was born. Called "rhythm 'n' blues" it combined the twenties classic blues style of Bessie Smith with the rhythmic impulses of boogie woogie and "shouts" of the Kansas City jazz style (George, 1988). It also embraced the European guitar by incorporating elements from the guitar-dominated country blues style of bluesmen like Robert Johnson and Big Bill Broonzy. In this way American country music, like the brass and reed band music of the jazz cycle, was combined with African elements and given new life. Louis Jordan led the way in R'n'B, which relied heavily on the new technology of radio for dissemination.

In the second decade, the 1950's, blacks began a new phase of political assertion with the Montgomery bus boycott and Brown v. The Board of Education. The struggle over the question of assimilation was epitomized by the tension between Martin Luther King and Malcolm X. The civil rights movement began a huge sweeping effort that would carry into the next decade. The seeds of the women's liberation movement were sown and, like civil rights, would explode in the sixties. Whites began to participate in the new music (Miller, 1980).

Many guitar playing country musicians of the time enjoyed R'n'B and were aware that the youth of the time were enamored by it. Numerous attempts were made to capture and exploit the "Negro sound" of Louis Jordan, Chuck Berry, Bo Diddley and others by combining it with country music. When Elvis finally succeeded, the rock 'n' roll revolution began. As in the jazz cycle, the church, parents, politicians, and all those with an investment in salvation and stability saw Elvis and his new music as vulgar, obscene, and dangerous. After all, "rock 'n' roll" was a euphemism for sexual intercourse. Of course Elvis' pelvic thrusts were really nothing new but only simple emulations of R'n'B moves that blacks had been performing for years. It was not the motions themselves that were the problem. What terrified white America was the infiltration of that libido into the mainstream culture on "The Ed Sullivan Show."

In 1957, one year after Elvis hit, Norman Mailer wrote an essay called "The White Negro" to describe whites "whose primary inspiration was the sexuality and music of Afro-Americans" (George, 1988, 61). This counterpart to the "white Negro" house slave was an albedo form of the white mind transformed by association with the blues. The black "white Negro" was changed by living in the house with the master; the white "white Negro" was changed by rhythm and blues. The intense passion for R'n'B felt by the white Negroes was the culmination of the blues seduction of the white mind. This passion was the collective psychological force that would break to bits the final remnants of the dying cultural consciousness of the West and establish the albedo in its place.

The second bacchanalia erupted in the 1960's. Those long-haired Dionysians, the Beatles, arrived from the East with their white minds transformed by the blues and sent massive throngs of pubescent maenads into frenzied hysteria. While it may seem odd that English rock'n'roll figured so heavily in this cycle, consider that the alchemy originally was set up in colonial America by the English. It was probably inevitable that this music would return to England, and eventually all of Europe, to transform its progenitors.

Exploiting the new technology of television, rock bands ignited a blast of hair, hippies, journeys back to the land, and "drugs, sex, and rock 'n' roll." This time, the participatory, bodily-felt oral consciousness that had been awakened in the jazz bacchanalia carried the problem of soul disenfranchisement to the point of overt cultural revolution. These young people had the "Truth" and that truth said "no" to the humiliating deadness of the materialistic establishment of their parents. Hugely inflated in the midst of their Dionysia, they advocated peace, love, and the virtuousness of open sexuality. Blacks, women, and youth fought together on the streets, not so much for overt political change but for a fundamental change in consciousness. "It has been said that the Beatles and Bob Dylan changed the musical and cultural consciousness of a whole generation. In this context it is important to realize that this great change of consciousness is based on the blues and would have been impossible without it" (Berendt, 137).

This bacchanalia saw the return of Dionysian religious experience which was foundational to the albedo. The widespread use of LSD during the sixties reflected a desire for ecstasy not salvation. These were "psychedelic" times that even manifest a musical form called "soul." Rather than fly upward toward spirit these revolutionaries wanted to go deeper into the soul-body intersection in a way imagined by all traditional blues players.

The 1970's were the tragic decade of the rock 'n' roll cycle. The peaceful Dionysia ended in death, addiction and cynicism. Hendrix, Joplin, and Morrison enacted the role of the young dying god. Woodstock led to Altamont. The Vietnam War ended and as Theseus was returning home Dionysos had his bride, and his father, Richard Nixon, took his own political life. However unexpected and bitter this tragic ending was for the youth, their revolution accomplished something gigantic—never again would the American Dream shine brightly enough to be believed.

Cycle Three: The Rap Revolution. In the 1980's yet another white backlash emerged in response to the gains made during the civil rights movement. The Reagan-Bush presidency was an attempt to assert once more the white supremacy of the economic fantasy. Affirmative action was attacked and the idea of "reverse discrimination" invented. Some blacks, mostly athletes and performers, had become very wealthy, which was both hated by supremacists but also used as a rationale by them to stop civil rights activities. Rap, a new music, was born (George, 1992; Ice T., 1994).

Rap was invented in the 1940's by radio announcers on R'n'B shows. They would speak rhythmically and in rhyme about themselves, their show, and the artists and music on the show. In the 1980's this talk was retrieved and combined with urban street rhythms and electric drum machines to create the dance music that is rap. As a narrative, the European form of rap appears to be joining and transforming its poetic drama. Indeed, the mythopoetic men's movement with its drumming, poetry, and story-telling owes much to rap and may be the concrete Western form that joins with it to create the new form of music. For in rap we hear what is perhaps the purest form of oral consciousness spoken in the West since Homeric Greece as well as the most fundamental representation of the unified orality that combines individual and communal consciousness. Of course, church and civic leaders hate rap, and parents are terrified of it.

As for its part in the return to materiality, rap has taken on what is probably the last great denial of the detached white mind in modernity. If jazz in the twenties brought back the body, and rock 'n' roll in the sixties brought back the soul, then rap today has brought back death. The youth gangs use this music of near pure rhythm to weave stories that accompany them on journeys of initiation, violence, and killing. We cannot deny death when young men and women die daily on our streets. Science turned the body into a dead corpse, not to honor Thanatos but to defeat him, or worse still, to tame him. But science has failed because Thanatos will not be tamed; he insists he will be honored and in our world the language that honors him is "gangsta" rap. However difficult it is for us to accept this music and the violent activity attached to it, it is clearly an extension of the return to materiality that started at the turn of the century with jazz. As we have come to recognize the gifts impacted in the tragedies of previous bacchanalias, the gifts of the return of body and soul, I believe we will come to recognize eventually a gift in rap in the return of death to our imaginations.

The 1990s is a decade in which blacks are again moving politically. The "Million Man March" of 1995 is a sign of this move. The issue of assimilation continues to be played out epitomized by the tension between Colin Powell and Louis Farakan. Whites are becoming involved in the rap of Snoop Doggy Dog, Dr. Dre, Ice T. and Arrested Development. It is very difficult to predict how this cycle will play itself out but it is certainly possible that rap will lead to yet another bacchanalia. If so, this bacchanalia will likely enact the death of Pentheus as gangs in the wilderness of our inner cities spill out into upscale neighborhoods and display the viciousness of a Dionysian episode in its final phase. Perhaps the alchemy will be completed in this cycle and with the albedo in place a polychromatic cultural soul will emerge.

Conclusion

In the end I find myself returning with near boundless awe the music itself. If my tale holds water then this soulful revolution, this massive cultural transformation, rests on the shoulders of twelve bars, three cords, and two lines of primitive verse originally sung in a most humble way by people on the bottom-most rung of our social ladder. What powerful shoulders they must be!

I am also in awe of the musicians. These African-Americans lived in conditions so horrid they were utterly destructive both physically and psychologically if experienced only literally. Yet these musicians were able to take a metaphoric and artistic stance toward their lives and in so doing answer our unconscious collective need by creating a language, a music that is capable of transforming the very white supremacist consciousness that spawned the horrid conditions in the first place. Civil rights and politics are good and necessary, but they seek change only on the level of the collective ego. It is the blues that does therapy on the soul of Western consciousness.

The white mind hunger for depression and the passions of the flesh, for embodied participation, could not be satisfied in a dissociative state. Likewise, mere acting out of depression and libido could not be enough. A psychologizing of the hunger was necessary if consciousness was to be changed and it is this imagining that such unassuming music was able to accomplish.

In the alchemy of race in America, the *unio mentalis* is a black man sitting on the porch playing a guitar and singing,

> Woke up this mo'nin', blues walkin' like a man.
> Woke up this mo'nin', blues walkin' like a man.
> Well de blues give me yo' right hand. (Johnson, 1990)

Works Cited

Berendt, J. *The Jazz Book*. Chicago: Lawrence Hill Books, 1982.

Cone, J. *The Spirituals and the Blues*. New York: Seabury Press, 1972.

Du Bois, W. E. B. *The Souls of Black Folks*. New York: Gramercy Books, 1994. (Originally published in 1903).

Finn, J. *The Bluesman*. London: Quartet Books, 1986.

Foster, W. Z. *The Negro People in American History*. New York: International Publishers, 1954.

George, N. *The Death of Rhythm and Blues*. New York: Plume Books, 1988.

George, N. *Buppies, B-boys, Baps, and Bohos*. New York: HarperCollins. 1992.

Hamilton, A. *The Hermes Complex: The Touchstone and the Postmodern Condition*. Unpublished manuscript, 1994.

Hillman, J. "Notes on White Supremacy." In *Spring 1986*, Dallas: Spring Publications, 1986.

Hillman, J. "Alchemical Blue and the *Unio Mentalis*." In *Spring 54*, Woodstock, Spring Publications, 1993.

Hughes, L. *Selected Poems*. New York: Vintage Classics, 1959.

Ice T. *The Ice Opinion*. New York: St. Martins Press, 1994.

Jung, C. G. *Memories, Dreams, and Reflections*. New York: Vintage Books, 1961.

Jones, L. *The Blues People*. New York: Morrow Quill Paperbacks, 1963.

Jacobson, R. *The Great Composers–Ludwig van Beethoven: His life and Times 1770-1804. Program Notes for the Sixth Symphony FW-301*. New York: Funk and Wagnalls, Inc., 1975.

Johnson, R. "Preachin' the Blues (Up jumped the Devil)." On, *Robert Johnson: The Complete Recordings.* (compact disk). New York: CBS Records, 1990. (Recorded in 1936 and 1937).

Kandinsky, W. *Concerning the Spiritual in Art.* New York: Dover Publications, 1971.

Lee, W. F. *Music Theory Dictionary.* New York: Charles Hansen Educational Music and Books, 1965.

Miller, D. "The self as no-self: Theoretical foundations of depth psychology in mystical theology." Paper presented at Pacifica Graduate Institute, Carpinteria, Calif., June, 1994.

Miller, J. (Ed.). *The Rolling Stone Illustrated History of Rock & Roll.* New York: Random House, 1980.

Murray, A. *Stomping the Blues.* New York: Da Capo Press, 1976.

Neumann, E. *Depth Psychology and a New Ethic.* Trans. Eugene Rolfe. Boston: Shambhala Publications, 1990.

Ogren, K. *The Jazz Revolution.* New York: Oxford UP, 1989.

Williams, P. J. *The Alchemy of Race and Rights.* Cambridge Mass.: Harvard UP, 1991.

[The author wishes to thank Robert Romanyshyn for his concept of post-literate oral consciousness which was central to the shaping of this work.]

COLOUR AS LANGUAGE AND SYMPTOM

JUDI BERTOIA

S oul language is not the mind's language. Rather, soul speaks through the affective and sensory, through metaphor and symbol, image and symptoms. In describing colour's capacity to produce impressions upon the soul, the painter Wassily Kandinsky (1977) compares words for colour such as red to words for musical instruments like trumpet. Their image and sound are audible to the soul in a manner distinct from sensory perception. While the words register with consciousness on one level, they also resonate more deeply with soul's immense cosmological awareness far beyond the capacity of language, in shades of colour and sound so fine in texture that they awaken inexpressible emotion in the soul. Kandinsky portrays human soul vibrations as deriving from an inner need, saying the language of colour, his grammar of painting, will only develop and be understood if it follows the rules of this inner need, the needs of the soul (35). However, soul's communication, this inner need manifest through psyche's multimodal and colourful directions, is usually poorly grasped by consciousness.

Judi Bertoia is a school counsellor with the Delta School Distric in Delta, British Columbia, Canada. She is the author of *Drawings from a Dying Child* (Routledge, 1993), and co-author, with John Allan, of *Written Paths to Healing* (Spring Publications, 1992).

Recently, the significance of colour as communication struck me when I realized how much I continue to be led in this work by children. As a Home/Hospital teacher many of my students were pregnant teens. Working with them developed into being a companion through the pain of giving up babies for adoption—grief work. A subsequent assignment involved working with critically ill children, many of whom died. One child in particular touched my life profoundly, becoming more my teacher than I ever was hers. She was aware of her prognosis, at first unconsciously and later consciously, even at age eight. She spoke of the presence and touch of her guardian angel and of having been to Heaven where the colours were so vivid, so pure. "There is no pollution in Heaven," was her explanation for the clarity of colour. She could also hear the angel's music. At first frightened by this, thinking they had come for her, she asked her mother to listen. Although her mother could hear the neighbor's wind chimes, this child's description was of something much richer, much fuller.

A child's fantasy? No, a deeper truth was presenting itself; soul was speaking through a child's voice, describing the colours and harmonies so present to poets, artists and those less encumbered by formal language, usually the very young, the seriously ill, the dying and the grieving.

Recently a healthy, established and respected adult colleague shared experiences that parallel this story. It would seem this individual is a bridge person, akin to shamans who communicate in some form with that same non-temporal realm. Baffled by most of what was shared from this spirit world, the individual was told understanding comes only when one can hear the colours sing. One must grasp the multiplicity and immensity of meanings directly from colour without the need for language. Intuitively and physiologically one must hear the vibrations in colours' song directly through soul, whether expressed in poppy red, tree green, or feeling blue. Kandinsky has a similar description: "Colour is a power which directly influences the soul. Colour is the keyboard, the eyes are the hammers, the soul is the piano with many strings" (25).

Multiple losses and deaths opened a communication pathway

from these friends for my colleague, just as death's proximity enhanced the child's capacity to experience sensory contact from that realm. Mogenson (1992) refers to individuals with this gift of receptivity, including C.G. Jung, and Marie-Louis von Franz (1984), and explores dreams and visions which demonstrate similar communication. Both Komp (1992) and Kübler-Ross (1983) also cite many examples of children experiencing dreams, the after-life and an intuitive awareness of soul's plan for them. These works make it clear that such encounters are "real." They take place not in recognized consensual reality but in the imaginal realm and in the unconscious corporeal body.

Acknowledging my strong connection to the dying student's drawings, yet unable to offer help, one professor suggested I train with Gregg Furth, a Jungian analyst who worked closely with Elisabeth Kübler-Ross. He in turn had studied extensively with Susan Bach, a London Jungian analyst who worked with the dying, especially children, and who had great expertise in the use of drawings as communication. All three of these companions to the dying see the power of image and colour to communicate (Bach, 1991; Furth, 1988; Kübler-Ross, 1983). All three see the capacity of psyche and soma, the body that we are, to dialogue within itself at a near mystical neurochemical level and to communicate within a broader imaginal field. How does this psyche/soma step out of our temporal existence to foretell what awaits? How does the hand use colour and image to draw an as yet undiagnosed illness? How does cosmological awareness send the newly-dead a continent away on an instantaneous visit telling a loved one about the physical death? Even knowing it happens, even having seen the drawings, even being told people's stories directly—almost as a relief that someone could be open to such an experience—even with all these, there is no explanation. There is only awe and the recognition that it does occur.

Perhaps this is why an exploration of colour can be so compelling; perhaps it is like an introduction to the scales of colour, a way of training or tuning receptivity to the songs of colour. While the thought of "hearing the colour" may be pure fantasy, a decade ago "reading a drawing," or experiencing synchronicity, or believing the stories told to Kübler-Ross were also the stuff of fiction. Now there is trust that undertaking the process is the important task whether it means learning the language of colour, image, words or combinations, not as a litany of interpretation, but simply entering the experience.

It seems as if Kandinsky, too, had considered such learning for he writes that both spirit and body can either be strengthened by frequent exercise or weakened if left untended. "The study of colour and its effects on men," he says, is the starting point for exercising spirit (36).

The Yoga tradition, too (Maheshwarananda, 1987), is based on the concept that the visible world, including colour, is but one element of many factors affecting human life. The cosmos contains countless forces streaming randomly in space and consists of powers that are invisible to the human eye—yet they form the true roots of humanity. When they concentrate into a single point a very strong energy force is created; the highest and strongest of those known to us is the human being. Through complex interactions of frequencies and vibrations the human being is physically embodied, mind and body, conscious and unconscious. Human *chakras*, literally wheels or vortices, resonate with different frequencies as do colours, feelings, sounds and visions. The sounds of ancient Sanskrit consist of particular tones and vibrations and this language itself is a manifestation of God vibrating on certain planes of the cosmos. These same planes exist in humans and are encoded within the body. Deep meditation on sound generates colours, the sacred letters, and *chakra* vibrations connected to sensations of cosmic forces, powers and qualities. Colour and sound thus become powerful bodily experiences of intense spiritual meaning.

The Resonance of Black

Communication is coloured by shades and hues on many deep levels, the words infiltrating our ordinary language and physical being with unconscious subtlety. For all people, Nature creates a universality; at the very least chlorophyll-green and blood-red are the pulsating life force of plants and animals everywhere. For each individual there is a personal relationship with colour; within each culture there are mythical, religious and traditional connections. Thus, humans experience multivalent responses to colour just as they do to images, and colours evoke an affective response, a reminder that physiology, emotion, and awareness are but an integrated part of the greater unity.

Black, the first colour in the alchemical process, is also the absorbing totality of the visible spectrum. Black light, an invisible frequency at the violet end of the colour spectrum, simply refers to ultraviolet rays. A black hole is an astronomical term for that which is so powerful it drags all energy into it. The term "Black Hole of Calcutta" is also used to indicate this suffocating nature, and although it refers historically to an infamous colonial imprisonment, common usage suggests even large numbers of people can vanish into the murky depth of oblivion. The patron deity of Calcutta is Kali, whose name means "black" (Elder, 1996). This dark goddess is akin to Europe's Black Madonna in that she can be seen as the dark and destructive side of humanity. The Black Madonna is also the earthy, embodied and beautifully feminine aspect of our spirituality; she has been retained for millennia, richly adorned and greatly honored through many cultures.

"Blackballed" or "blacklisted" implies rejection by a group, and being the "black sheep of the family" suggests either rejection by or rebellion against that family. The "black hand" indicates being marked for death within a secret society subculture. Reminders of human frailty include the black plague or "black death," the black widow's sting and miners' "black lung," while the superficial vanity of beautiful skin is marred by blackhead pimples. "Blackmail" is extortion under the threat to expose some damaging past act. Stock markets crash on "Black Friday" and "Black Monday." Selling goods on the "black market" is usually illegal, yet being "in the black" indicates business is operating healthily. "Black gold" describes oil, the major lubricant of modern financial culture.

"Blacktop" provides surfacing for highways world-wide, but when covered in "black ice," as so often happens in less temperate zones, travel becomes treacherous. "Black rain" signals the damage of modern technology polluting natural processes, yet nature's resiliency shows in the weed-like tenacity of plants such as Black-eyed Susans and blackberries or the determined perseverance of the black beetle, cockroaches. The Black Forest is home to cuckoo clocks, health spas and great natural beauty but also carries many other images in fairy tales. So, too, the "black rose," such a deep violet it appears black, generates multiple layers of associations. Even though they are usually green now, schools still have blackboards in every room and modern air transport requires a "black box" on every flight.

Depression, a "black mood," or being pursued by the "black dogs" of myth is a well recognized state ind its symptoms are fully listed in the *DSM IV*, psychology's "black book." Despair is also thought of as blackness, filling a hopeless "black pit." Being under a "black cloud" suggests an irritable mood or being under suspicion, while singing "Bye-Bye, Blackbird" resonates with attempts to shrug off this mantle of gloom. A black eye is a sign of violence or shame, and a bruised ego indicates a wounding, a psychic state of being "black and blue."

"Black of night" implies an unknown, shadowy quality that can make people uneasy and worried for their safety. Being kept in the dark suggests little control, for others are not forthcoming with information. "Keeping to the shadows" implies remaining unseen by intention. It is our shadow or dark side that intimidates as much as our instinctual concern for survival. Violent behavior often takes place under cover of darkness, as if our human nature is more readily discarded or camouflaged in poor light. The Ninja assassins of Japan found darkness an ally in hiding their presence.

Choice of colour is often used for group identification such as a biker's black leather jacket, gang colours, or a team name, like hockey's Chicago Black Hawks. "Black Irish" is a slang used for Dublin's tough inner city lads. A black arm-band was also used to indicate solidarity with imprisoned IRA members on a hunger strike in the 1980s. In recent American history the Black Panthers became a strong, militant voice. The Gestapo's choice of black uniforms to intimidate is one indicator of the capacity to use colour as an aid in asserting or abusing power. "The Black Shirts" of Italy, also a term for Nazi "SS" members, is another example of colour used for dictatorial powers run amok. Corruption of the humane as well as the physical body are often associated to black. Blackbeard's murderous brutality is legendary. Historically the wearing of black clothing or a black arm band has indicted mourning, and in many cultures women are obligated to wear black either as widows or simply as women. It is interesting to note that ancient Egyptians viewed the darker Ethiopians as inferior and even today the diminished status of women in many fundamentalist Muslim societies is marked by black clothing.

In western culture, a black tie marks the formality of social occasions and the essential "little black dress" finds approval at most functions. A "black belt" in karate marks its highest achievement and expert status. "Black humor" helps survival in difficult circumstances. "Black power" and "black pride" reflect a positive outgrowth of this culture's historical view of black as inferior. Black as the "Ace of Spades" could be either an insulting description or a reference to the mysterious and unsettling quality of total darkness. The combination of black's elegant sophistication and velvet's soft smoothness is so strong an image that it has even been adopted as a trade name for whiskey. Black prairie soil and black compost are the most fertile because old material, fully exposed and de-composed, provides a richness of nutrients for sustaining new growth. Getting one's hands dirty implies working this soil or other physical labor in demanding bodily involvement, but it may also suggest a lower social status as one who lacks the aristocratic breeding, wealth or mastermind capabilities to direct others. Eating "black bread" would have similar implications in the past.

A "blackout" may indicate the loss of electrical power or the covering of light sources to remain undetected by an enemy; but "blacking out" is internal, a loss of consciousness or ego awareness. A time of inner darkness is usually unpleasant, but can also become a time of interiority, a valued visit to the unconscious depths. For the feminine it may even be necessary since, like Persephone and Inanna, the feminine needs a time of withdrawal and isolation from the world to integrate shadow aspects if further development is to occur, especially at mid-life. Yet this development of feminine strength is also associated with power from the unconscious realm and historically has come to be associated with witches. Such relationship derives in part from the black clothing worn by mature women and widows, referred to in slang as "black crones" or "black crows." A witch's familiar, the black cat, is thought to bring bad luck when crossing one's path. Black capes, hoods and masks carry a connection to witches, vampires, Thanatos, and the disguise of the executioner. Thus, black may connote the sinister.

Black magic, too, implies a power or control by another realm, feared as coming from the dark side. *Star Wars* character, Darth Vader's total blackness epitomizes the human capacity to be turned to destructive uses of power and technology. The black horses and black chariot of Hades are considered ominous signs, hinting at being abducted into this underworld. The nigredo of the alchemical process refers to the chaos of the *prima materia*, contained only by the vaguest sense of primordial darkness or the "Void." It is a time of not seeing and not knowing, an absence of light and enlightenment. Melancholy and death are part of this stage, a roasting or charring of the material. Few voluntarily enter this domain, yet there is also an unspoken relationship to being born anew. Just as Dante went through Hell before reaching Paradise, modern man often experiences the rich depths of blackness before emerging with a renewed relationship to soul.

Conclusion

Steven Spielberg's movie *Close Encounters of the Third Kind* portrays contact with aliens. Initially through one-way communication, aliens contact receptive human adults and children. In one opening scene an old man who had witnessed the brilliant multi-coloured lights of their space ship says, "The sun came out last night. It sang to me." At one point, as colours and music haltingly co-ordinate an intergalactic jitterbug, one man comments, "They're trying to teach us a basic tonal vocabulary." The vivid technicolour conclusion is a dialogue between this advanced species and humanity through variegated colour in sophisticated ballet with complex, computer-enhanced music. This communion is enriched by sign language, the gestural body simplifying soul meaning in direct, poignant contact. The resolution contains bittersweet joy for there is two-way interaction and mutual choice in maintaining the connection. Such an ending balances the underlying chaos for those who feel crazy as a result of initial contact, and reassures some of those who fear that which is alien. Childhood innocence is not so much lost as reinforced. It is the child-like openness that engages a complex colour/sound channel, calling the aliens on the coloured keys of a toy xylophone and later facilitating communication for others.

Can we learn the songs of our own alien nature through colour? Can we develop a dialogue with those who inhabit our own imaginal realms, those who are compelled to speak through symptom because we have forgotten or cannot hear the language of soul? Another line from this movie reflects the struggle to stand aside the bias which says all this is fantasy, "It's all coincidence. It's not scientific." Yet Spielberg and Kandinsky, and my student and my colleague have all manifest similar content, four diverse souls communicating essentially the same message through vastly different experiences.

It is possible that we must each develop our own soul circuitry to embrace the music and metaphor, colour and concepts offered so willingly yet so incomprehensibly to our everyday awareness. The ghosts and angels, dream figures and inner voices are present; they resonate within the energy fields we, too, inhabit. Somehow they touch us deeply first, but only slowly do the ripples surface. Just as each colour has its own wavelength, perhaps these others seek our ability to register their spectrum, to be en-lightened by them and to listen to them, communicating in energy patterns we barely perceive.

Works Cited

Bach, S. *Life Paints its Own Span: On the Significance of Spontaneous Pictures by Severely Ill Children.* Einsiedeln, Switzerland: Daimon Verlag, 1990.

Furth, G. M. *The Secret World of Drawings: Healing through Art.* Boston: Sigo Press, 1988.

Elder, G. R. *The Body: An Encyclopedia of Archetypal Symbolism.* Boston: Shambhala Publications, 1996.

Kandinsky, W. *Concerning the Spiritual in Art.* Trans. M. T. H. Sadler. New York: Dover Publications, Inc, 1977.

Komp, D. M. *A Window to Heaven: When Children See Life in Death.* Grand Rapids: Zondervan Publishing House, 1992.

Kübler-Ross, Elizabeth. *On Children and Death.* New York: Macmillan Publishing Company, 1983.

Maheshwaranada, P. S. *The Path of Consciousness.* Trans. Swami Gitananda Puri, Vienna: Austrian-Indian Yoga-Vedanta Society, 1987.

Mogenson, Greg. *Greeting the Angels: An Imaginal View of the Mourning Process.* Amityville, New York: Baywood Publishing Company, Inc., 1992.

Von Franz, Marie-Louise. *On Dreams and Death.* Boston: Shambhala Publications, Inc., 1984.

The Garden and the Gods: Life from the Haitian Perspective

HENRY HOGARTH

I believe that past and present conditions in the United States and Haiti have bound both people through their cultures in an alchemical opus, much like two individuals who are simultaneously attracted and repelled by each other. In returning to Haiti with such an overwhelming display of force, the West, via the United States and the United Nations, is "unconsciously" meeting its historical shadow; in "inviting" the Great White, Haiti, like Jonah, enters the belly of the whale to be born again. Both cultures are fast coming up on historically significant dates: Haiti's independence bicentennial is to be celebrated in the year 2004, while the West's eschatology has the End of its World (or of its Bible, as some polytheists think)[1] occurring at around the same period.

Born in Port-au-Prince, Haiti, Henry Hogarth was educated in New York in the Sixties. For the past ten years, he has lived in Miami where he has been an interpreter/translator of French, Kreyol, and English. He recently moved back to Haiti where he now resides. He is writing a book entitled, *The Land of Kham*, a treatment of Ancient Egyptian theology, Vodou and the New Millenium.

Thus, as countries so opposed in psychology come in closer "body" contact (Haitian immigration/American invasion), their collective psyches likewise touch. In a strange but understandable twist, Haitians turn to Protestantism in greater numbers while more and more Americans become atheists or "born again pagans." However, before we can begin to imagine what dynamic and creative synergy, if any, might develop out of this encounter, we will first have to look at the way African customs and beliefs pervade the entire Haitian culture.

The most telling expression used by traditional, rural Haitians that describes the inherent separateness between themselves and the urban dwellers is : *m'ap tounen andeyò*—I'm returning *outside*. No less significant is : *m' pral nan peyi'm*—literally, I'm going to my country, meaning, of course, I'm going home. Both expressions indicate the sense that the Haitian countryman or woman has in regards to what is considered home, "country": the hills, the plains, the valleys of the rural area. Home is definitely not the city. One might even infer that the average Haitian countryman does not relate much to the notion of Haiti as nation-state or *res publica*.[2]

From this perspective, the major achievement of the Haitian revolution, though one certainly not intended by the Founders of that republic, was the creation of a society functioning outside of, if not quite against, the State. That society was not, and is not, a subculture. It embodies the dominant culture, dominant in the sense that, although denied, repressed, alienated and vilified by the elite, both national and foreign, it remains the "ground" of Haiti's essence. It provides the soulfulness one finds in Haitian art, for instance.

Being the inheritors of the ancient African tradition which has sustained their spirit, in spite of all the attacks both from within and without, the people of the "country outside" struggle to find their way. Recently, for many, it has meant emigrating to foreign, often hostile shores for reasons of economic survival. For others, it means remaining in Haiti, surviving and believing that "*Bondyé bon*"—God is good. It is this culture and the mindset of these people that I will now present.

THE GARDEN AND THE GODS 63

Peyi Andeyò: The New World's Counterculture.

Historians generally agree that the movement which lead to Haiti's independence from France started in the year 1791 and advanced after a *Vodu* "service" that took place August 15, 1791 at Bwa Kayiman, in the northern part of Haiti. The ceremony marked the end of a congress of guerrilla leaders that convened in order to coordinate their various bands of maroons. The ceremony is said to have been conducted to call upon the gods, asking them to assist the Africans in their fight for freedom. History books tell of a night of lightning and thunder, drums and dancing, during which a solemn oath was taken by all those attending to "Live free or die." After thirteen years of political and military maneuvering by erstwhile French but black colonial army leaders such as Toussaint Louverture, Dessalines, Christophe and Petion, Haiti was declared an independent black nation.[4]

The end of colonial rule achieved, the convergence of both classes of Haitians quickly gave way to a gradual rift as both realized they each had different political, economic and social agendas. The plantations in the richest colony of the Western world, now in the hands of former warlords and their mercantilist allies, still required heavy labor: how were they to remain prosperous if the bulk of former slaves were now free men and women, occupying their own land and toiling for themselves and their families?

In a manner similar to apartheid, but without the outright racism, the Creole rulers of the day, (i.e., those born on the colonial soil), tried to reinstitute forced field labor, albeit without chains. Needless to say this did not sit well with the Africans. More and more, the lower class migrated further and further away from the plains and into the mountains, there to live as their ancestors had: in their gardens with their gods.[5]

After independence, the men and women living *andeyò*, as far away from town and cities as possible, established their difference from the colonials and the Creoles. They were not concerned with the establishment of a state nor with a suitable form of government and definitely not interested in the paraphernalia involved; constitutions, government appointments, responsibilities and entitlements, and elections. All this left the majority of these former slaves indifferent. In fact, independence to them meant exactly that. Furthermore, while they knew and understood that agricultural production was exported to the outside world and that commerce made people rich and powerful, they never had the desire to engage in trade with foreigners. At most, when they needed something made from a town merchant's store, they would barter or sell whatever they had brought down from the hills in exchange for what they needed and made their way back home as soon as possible. This behavior that be still observed in Haiti today.

Right from the start then, money and power were considered and treated differently by the African society *qua* state. Since they were not legally forbidden to export products or to participate in government, we must assume that such behavior was voluntary and collective. But, there were also other factors that helped define what was becoming a noticeable aspect of the "national" character.

As early as 1843 a foreign author of the day remarked that "having no acquired needs, they experience no frustration." In 1832, a Haitian writer named Beaubrun Ardouin wrote that "the sobriety of the people of the rural areas, particularly, is such that very little effort is needed to satisfy primary needs; thus the nonchalance one notices amongst these inhabitants towards subjecting themselves to assiduous and regular work that would considerably increase the current products." More telling is the opinion of the Haitian President, Stenio Vincent, speaking a hundred years later in 1938 about the same rural inhabitant : "The man is ignorant, superstitious, *without needs*, with dissolute habits, without a taste for work, left to himself and to the bad instincts of his nature, going about with almost no clothes, apparently without being the least embarrassed 'wasting the land'"[6]

While we have no known written record in the early period (after 1804) to tell us what the new Haitians living *andeyò* thought like, we do have the modern remnants of the tradition which enveloped and sustained them, and continues to this day. Contrasting sharply with the Western scientific view, "the religious behavior of the [Haitian] peasant cannot be conceived of in terms of the domination of his milieu. Symbolically, the *Lwa* [gods] have invested the natural environment of their presence by contagion, nature, thus spiritualized, affirms its spiritual dimension, beyond the reach and power of man."[7] Since there were no documents written by these new Haitians, it is a matter of conjecture whether one is willing to attribute speculative powers and pragmatic reasoning, or lack thereof, to the founders of this society. Certainly they had a "body of thought," a set of core beliefs, feelings, attitudes, a sure sense of who they were and of the way things were/are/ought to be.

Political philosophy/theory/ideology existing in these early years is also a question. What the African leaders think about before and after the war? The fact that they were often assassinated by the Creole military leadership, who were about to restructure a pseudo-modern state based on a cash crop export concept of economic exchange, (something like the prevailing forms of social organization in western Europe)[8] indicates that they posed some threat to the urban statesmen.

A*ndeyò* was a social structure named the *lakou*, an important concept in their development. If we consider the plantation as the representative element of what colonialism was in terms of sociology, economy and politics, then the *lakou* is its systemic antithesis. Against the impersonality of the plantation supervisor was now the venerable patriarch. Around his house were those of his many wives. (Each wife was referred to as *manman pitit* to establish the difference between her and his common law wife, who lived in the main house.) Not too far from these homes was the *kay mistè*, the house of the "mysteries," the gods, the *Lwa*. A little further away were those of his children and their wives, and in the outlying area, the *jaden* or gardens These gardens were portions of land received by the original parents at the time of the national redistribution of land following the Revolution. And, always close by, are the tombs of family members and relatives.[10]

Since farming these pieces of land often required more than one person's labor and when the immediate family members were still not enough, others, usually neighbors from around the area, were asked to help. Here again an African custom was revived: non-salaried collective work - the *kombit*. Because work is the base of human activity, the *kombit* is the *modus operandi* which defines the socioeconomic structure in Haitian rural society.

In their rejection of colonialism at the beginning of the nineteenth century, the Haitians were turning away from industrialism and the machine which were quickly becoming the way and means of European development. Capitalism and democracy, as cultural superstructures, evolved in the opposite direction of the agrarian, theocratic synarchy which constituted the *peyi andeyò*. Their specific cultural behaviors were established early and mark the real, unstated revolution which took place. Their revolution was in advance of socialism without having been initiated by Marx. It upended the notion of the Hegelian state as the embodiment of reason as well. The Haitian independence, seen from the African point of view, was a formal, systemic opposition to the norm of the day, both in the towns and cities of Haiti and outside of it. It carried forward the situation that Haiti finds itself today. As a result, Haiti is far outside the Western mainstream and has earned itself the title the "poorest nation of the Western hemisphere."

An Archaic Mentality

One accomplishment of Haitian society, although admittedly forced, was the creation of a new language: *Kreyòl*.[12] It is not clear whether this language was preexistent to their arrival and deriving from an admixture of Northern French dialects with little African input or whether it was put together by the slaves themselves to facilitate communication between the various ethnic groups hearing French being spoken, or whether a confluence of both. The content of the language, its "spirit," yields insight into the psychology that textures the Haitian culture.

When confronting a perplexing situation requiring a difficult decision, a Haitian will sometimes ponder a moment and then say: "*Lide'm di'm' Lwa.*" Translated literally, this means "my idea tells me. . ." In another instance, if a Haitian is pressed to give an explanation as to why whatever may have been expected of him/her has not been done, a Haitian might answer: "*paske lide'm pa di'm fe'l.*" This phrase signifies, depending on the tone in which it was said, either a willful, self-induced decision *not* to do whatever was asked or expected, or it might mean, as in the English expression "something tells me. . .," "I have an idea that you are asking me to do what I'm not comfortable with."

What is significant, I find, is the use of "idea" to cognize something other than "I." There is an expression denoting willful intent: "*m'pa vlé*"—"I don't want"—but it is used more often in simple cases of dislike or refusing something offered, proposed, or suggested. For instance, instead of "I don't want to do this," one might hear, "my idea doesn't tell me to"—*m'pa vle fe'l 'lidé'm pa di'm*. It is as though the person "wills" the option suggested by his "*lide.*" In a sense, the "*lide*" can be considered as a psychic function such as intuition.

Such expressions reveal the traditional Haitian's psychological, perhaps even psychic, awareness of a prompting which originates from another domain, realm, or dimension.[13] At the very least, in their language, Haitians establish the vividness of consciousness, or, if one prefers, the "aliveness of soul" which is the *sine qua non* condition of the rural Haitian mentality. "Even nowadays, when we try to recapture the past, we may lose sight of our own share in an event in which we were once implicated, and ask ourselves: how did this plan or that thought ever come to me? If we take this notion, that a thought 'came' to us, and give it a religious twist, we come fairly close to the Homeric attitude."[14]

The body is viewed in the Haitian countryside as a thing apart and different from one's self. When greeting one another in the morning, the rural Haitians say: "*ki jan ou ye? e kò a?*"— "How are you? And your body?" In the day to day world, this is a way of inquiring about one another's health. Since much depends on having a fit and healthy body to perform the day's labor in an agrarian culture such as Haiti's, the body's specific cultural importance is understandable.

In a wider cultural perspective, however, in what could be called the metaphysical dimension, the body is known and referred to as *kadavkò*, literally the cadaver-body or corpse. How this contradiction fits within the general psychology of *Vodu* and how it ties in with ancient Egyptian concepts about the soul, life and death (afterlife), is observable in the relationship between what is known as *gwobonzanj, ti bonzanj* (guardian angel, little guardian angel) and the *kadavkò,* in being human. The knowledge of this interrelationship is nowhere better demonstrated than in the "living dead" phenomenon known as *zombi*.[15]

Other culturally distinctive linguistic expressions merit comment as well. To describe the inner dialogue or running conversation one sometimes has with one's self, *en aparté*, is rendered thus in *Kreyòl*: "*nan kè'm m'di...*"—in my heart I said..."For Homeric man, the *thymos*, defined roughly as the organ of feeling, tends not to be felt as part of the self: it commonly appears as an independent inner voice"[16] located in the chest or midriff. The urbanized Haitian, having been "educated" through a Westernized pedagogy that reinforces the cerebral and intellectual mode of perception, will voice the same inner experience by saying: "*m'di tèt mwen...*"—"I said to my head." "If, as we have suggested, *thymos* is the mental organ which causes (e)motion, while *noos* is the recipient of images, then *noos* may be said generally to be in charge of intellectual matters, and *thymos* of things emotional."[17]

By the time of Socrates, the inner voice had become a "personal" *daemon* which, allowing for cultural transposition, could today be assimilated, without much discrepancy of function, to whatever god is the "master of the head" (*lwa mèt tèt*) of the *sèvitè* in *Vodu*. The "headmaster" is the god that most often appears to him in dreams to advise, admonish or inform. In modern times, what was once felt/known/perceived as *thymos* and *noos* in Homeric times could, as abstracted entities, easily be equated with the Jungian psychic functions of intuition and intellect.

Perhaps more determinant psychologically than any single linguistic factor is the lack of a Creole expression translating the self-affirmative, existentially emphatic "I am" of Descartes' *cogito, ergo sum*. It would have to be *"mwen ye"* or *"m'ye."*[18] We find instead the expression *"m'se"* which establishes self definition by relatedness as in *"m'sé pitit entel"*—"I am such and such's child," or *"m'se doktè entèl"*—"I am doctor so and so." Also of note is that there is no linguistic distinction between "we" and "you" (plural) as in "we are happy that all of you were able to come"— *"nou kontant nou tout te ka vini."* Both "we" and "you" are expressed by the same word — *nou*. The alterity of the other(s) is not expressed. Thus we might surmise, it is not psychologically acknowledged in the collective body that which remains: "we." There is of course in the Creole language an "I" (*mwen or m'*), a "you" (singular) (*ou*) and a "they" (yo).[19] This lack of emphasis on the self as a distinctly felt "I am" ego is at the foundation of the sociology of *andeyò* as well as the cornerstone of its psychology.

The Psychology of Vodu

> At all events, we stand between two worlds [North-South] or between two totally different systems of perception; between perception of external sensory stimuli and perception of the unconscious. The picture we have of the outer world makes us understand everything as the effect of physical and physiological forces; the picture of the inner world shows everything as the effect of spiritual agencies.[20]

Haiti has a world view based on *psyche* whereas Western culture is based on *techne*. Where Haiti values tradition, psychological and subjective experience as a way of "knowing," in the Western world it is innovation, technological and objective experimentation that is valued. Haiti has complex rites and rituals that proffer the invisible and intangible as real. In the Western imagination sensible, hard facts, the of the mechanics of matter in motion, mathematics and complex and abstract formulas are "real." The importance of the group, the extended family, and the community (comprised of both the living and dead) in Haiti is in sharp contrast to the Western emphasis on the individual, the nuclear family and the corporate team.[21]

The Africans that were brought to the part of Haiti that was part of the French colony of Saint-Domingue were mainly from the West coast of Africa. These Africans had lived in their homeland in well-organized kingdoms. Despite the ethnic diversity sometimes found within African kingdom there were enough common cultural and religious features among them to enable a synthesis of view and practice by the slaves even before Haitian independence had been achieved. Such is *Vodu*.[22] While *Vodu* allowed for a wide array of rites, rituals, and rhythms inherited from the different *nanchons*, (nations, i.e., ethnic groups)[23] their differentiated but common gods merged into the recognizable "nuclear" patterns of the major *Lwa*. *Vodu* forms an integrated, "holistic" system, not of worship but of energy transformation.[24] It enabled the enslaved Africans to free themselves from France's colonial rule by providing the motivation and the means, both physical (poison) and psychic (possession), to wage war. Subsequently, it provided the Africans who were now in possession of Haiti with the background necessary to establish a society in the New World, one based on different concepts of self and society than that of Europe.

Chief among the features shared by early Haitians was the pervasive propitiation of the gods and of the ancestors by and through a working knowledge of archetypal powers at play and at work. This identifiable characteristic of African culture is first evident in Ancient Egypt: the first known culture to have recorded "in stone" the birth and death of gods and the rituals whereby humankind might participate of their essence in this life and the hereafter. "Egypt was as much a land of gods as of men, and the inhabitants of the country wherein the gods lived and moved naturally devoted a considerable portion of their time upon earth to the worship of the divine beings and of their ancestors who had departed to the land of the gods."²⁵

In psychological terms, since "psychic processes antedate, accompany, and outlive consciousness," and since "consciousness is an interval in a continuous psychic process,"²⁶ "we may establish with reasonable certainty that an individual consciousness as it relates to ourselves has come to an end. But whether this means that the continuity of the psychic process is also interrupted remains doubtful, since the psyche's attachment to the brain can be affirmed with far less certitude today than it could fifty years ago."²⁷ Haitian culture is analphabetical. The traditional Haitian sees and knows his story as the story of the ancestors, of the *Lwa*, as a living memory rooted in the community and its members in the timeless principles and archetypes that govern life and death, condition character, and mold behavior. As active agents in this reciprocal process, traditional Haitians the that relate to them become, to use Maya Deren's expression, "divine horsemen." Humans are not merely personalities affected or "infected" by archetypes whose influence have a "disturbing effect on the ego."

> In *Vodun* the cosmic drama of man consists not of a dualism, a conflict of the irreconcilable down-pull of flesh and the up-pull of spirit; it is, rather, an almost organic dynamic, a process by which all that characterizes divinity—intelligence, power, energy, authority, wisdom—evolves out of the flesh itself. Instead of being eternally separated, the substance and the spirit of a man are eternally and mutually committed: the flesh to the divinity within it and the divinity to the flesh of its origin.²⁸

Living one's life, then, is more than a "going until the end of allotted time on earth." Though my life is marked by the passage of time, the living of it is a creation in that it is primarily within my psychic involvement that the gods and the dead have their being. By remembering them, I remember myself and make myself whole so that I may not die a second time. "In the divinity and the immortality of the god-man Osiris lay the strength of the power with which he appealed to the minds and hopes of the Egyptians for thousands of years... both these concepts of Osiris are of purely African origin and were in existence long before the dynastic period in Egypt."[29]

> Many Haitians hold that every infant is born with a *mait tete*—a spirit who is the "master of the head" while the "inherited *loa*" are usually not the personal deities but the special protectors of the household or the *hounfor* and are known as "*loa* of the house" or "family *loa*."[30]

The vital contact of the *servitè* with his "daemon," *genius natalis* or *lwa mèt tèt*, (that is, his dynamic association with an unseen, informing "headmaster") is the objective purpose of *Vodu kay* or "*Vodu* of the household." *Vodu kay* is the attention and care given to personal *Lwa* and the family cult given to the family ancestors; the personal *Lwa*, the family ancestors and the family *lwas* constitute the family *mambre*,[31] the divine genealogy of the family tree. For the Haitian, it is family heritage that is the source of life force, it is story that equips the Haitian for life, and it is from the ancestral *loa* that the psychic energy and intelligence from which empowerment and instruction in daily life is derived.[32] The *mèt tèt*, coalesced from archetypes, constitutes a personal, individuated nucleus around which all the other psychic manifestations will be "incorporated."

Awareness of the archetypal is demonstrable. The *manbre*, a "psychoid" conglomerate of personal and extended family ancestors, includes the particular *lwas* served in the family and the *sevitè*'s head master. In the home *rogatwa*,[33] this partially collective psychic ancestry is tended through conversations with the invisible forms which comprise it and with prayers and libations to representations of Christian saints that have become the icons of the *lwa*. These entities, or mental images, or "partial personalities," are sustained both by tradition and personal practice. The numinous and natural authority they bear is seen in the veneration accorded these *eidolons* from generation to generation, knowledge and awareness of them are the responsibility of parents and are the very essence of the *Vodu* tradition. "Our images are our keepers, as we are theirs."[34]

The protective relationship provided by the *Lwa* is the traditional objective of the *lave tèt,* literally, head washing. "The main effect of the *laver-tete* is to establish a permanent link between the neophyte and a *loa*. In ritual language, this ceremony corresponds with the placing of the *loa mait-tet* (the *loa* master of the head). From then on the novice is consecrated to one particular spirit who will be his protector... In Haiti no *loa* claim a monopoly. Despite the rights a *mait-tet* holds over his servant he does not take offense when another *loa* uses his 'horse.'"[35]

As member of a social body, every Haitian is "psychically grounded." This includes his family ancestors through a wide web of extended families, *sosyete* (society), and work groups. This is enhanced by participation in a collective the *Vodu peristil* that holds ceremonial dances to which everyone and anyone is welcome and that take place according to a yearlong liturgical calendar. "You are with the divine only as far as you are communal."[36] "If a family fails to have the *met-tet* of one of its members properly removed at death, it may be persecuted afterward by the spirit of the dead ancestor and by the *loa* as well."[37] So, special collective feasts are often held in honor of the dead, familial and national.

Thus, a different kind of "ego complex" and consciousness evolves in the Haitian living *andeyò*. Aware at an early age of the vivid reality of the invisible, he or she acknowledges intertwining of the dead, the living and the intermediaries between himself and the Absolute One Great God which, as a *sevitè*, is referred to as *gran mèt*. The four realms (the invisible with/in the mineral, the vegetal, the animal) operates through ritualized "psychic"/animic interaction. As a *sèvitè* or "servant of the gods," a Haitian is literally their host whenever there is a foodfest (*manje Lwa*) held in their honor. Conditioned early on through this all inclusive approach to reality, a Haitian knows that there are forces greater than him or herself that are part of everyone and everything around him.[38]

"The whole of the social fabric of Egypt rested upon religious principles of the most absolute character, and the foundation of them all was the cult of the ancestral spirit, or ancestral god."[39] We have already seen how, *andeyò*, the "spiritualization" of the traditional Haitian begins early with the installation of the *mèt tèt*, the nuclear pattern of psychic energy with which/whom he will entertain a serious, intimate rapport throughout life. At death, and for awhile thereafter, parents and friends of the family will make sure that both he and his head-master *lwa* are appeased since the deceased will be called upon many times to assist the living. The dead in Haiti do not sleep or "rest in peace." In Haiti "a dead person is spoken of as though he had survived himself in the form of disembodied soul."[40] He is spoken to as well.

While life in the hereafter is a belief shared by many cultures, in Haiti's *andeyò*, death, burial, the passage to the other side are practical matters dealing with the reality of "soul stuff." They are not merely symbolic ceremonials of remembrance. We are dealing with real concern about "living" where "the underworld is the mythological style of describing a psychological cosmos."[41] How does one survive there then? For the most part, by ensuring that the *mèt tèt* and the *gwobonzanj* are once more separated.

"The *gros/bon/ange* is the metaphysical double of the physical being...it is the immortal twin who survives the mortal man... the *gros/bon/ange*, as the repository of a man's history, his form and his force, the final resultant of his ability, intelligence and experience, is a precious accumulation."[42] "The *ti/bon/ange* requires the least ritual labor. Indeed it is characteristic of the anonymous, transcendent, spiritual nature of the *ti/bon/ange* that it is automatically liberated at the moment of death and hovers over the body for nine days before ascending to heaven... it is, in a sense, the objective, impersonal, spiritual component of the individual. In the rites of the dead, it plays no role."[43]

"To that part of man which beyond all doubt was believed to enjoy a special existence . . . the Egyptians gave the name *ba*, a word which means something like 'sublime,' 'noble,' and which has always hitherto been translated by "soul." The *ba* is not incorporeal, for although it dwells in the kha, and is . . . the principle of life in man, still it possesses both substance and form..."[44] We have a commingling of substances constituting what in Christian culture have been termed "soul" and "spirit," both of which have been the object of speculation and controversy in Western literature, sacred and secular.[45]

The problem that arises here is our desire to continue dealing with these psychological processes as though they were nothing but "mythological projections," thus not real, happening in the "heads" of various individuals of a particularly remote epoch. However, it is difficult not to realize as well that if these processes are attended to by others, they must be occurring in a dimension collectively known and perceived. Moreover the fact that they are inherited, "inwardly" through the invisibles and "outwardly" through the rites, establishes their field relations (to use an expression from physics). That virtually the same processes occurring in Haiti today occurred in Egypt more than 5000 years ago can be seen as proof positive that, although intangible, the collective invisible is alive and real.

In this light, *Vodu* is not a faith or a dogmatic "religion" founded by a great individual possessing the Truth, unless he was Osiris himself. Nor is it meditative mysticism. In its effort to combat it, the Christian Church has always imagined the African, the perennial *sèvitè*, as a devil worshipper and an apostate of the true faith, possession being the obvious proof. But if "faith is the complete receptivity and self-surrender of the intellect to the Unseen and Unknown,"[46] who could be more truly faithful than the *sèvitè of vodu*? *Vodu* is not a Gnosis either, although "it seems as though some Gnostics, at least, came very near to understanding the archetypes as psychoid, that is, subliminal, collective, autonomous energy quanta, manifesting typically in synchronistic or transcendental experiences, possessing individuals and operating through them."[47] While "humanistic psychotherapies are based on the assumption that humanity has become too intellectual, technologized, and detached from sensations and emotions...they emphasize experiential, nonverbal, and physical means of personality change . . ."[48] "'Well then, come and dance,' says the *sèvitè*: 'those who dance not, know not what cometh to pass. Amen. . . Understand by dancing what I do.'"[49]

Vodu is a superstition (and rightly so, in the original Latin meaning of the term) of ancient knowledge about the nature of the soul. It is, as a way of living, a practical application of principles preserved in a tradition outlined about three thousand years before the Christian era and one that allows the experience of a more "psychologically conscious" relationship with the transpersonal.

Vodu is here considered as archetypal psychology *ab origine,* whose ritualized "lay practice" by any *sèvitè* of the gods becomes a therapeutic process of living, (i.e., interacting with the dead and the deep, with the personal, familial and collective unconscious). Therapy becomes theater and progress, possibly a pilgrimage to the primitivism of the pagan *peristyle.* "The barbarian may be at the gate because the empire has decayed from within. He may even come to voice well-justified grievances which, for the good of our souls, we dare not ignore."[50] Trance 'n' dance!

Notes

[Editor's Note: Mr. Hogarth has supplied the reader with lengthy notes which are essential to understanding his essay. However, some of the references are incomplete in that they do not provide the names of publishers and the publication dates. It was impossible for us to reach Mr. Hogarth in Haiti to make these additions. We hope that the information provided here is enough to help anyone interested in further research.]

[1] "It is the Apocalypse of the *Bible* ... the Bible is over, not the world." James Hillman. *We've Had a Hundred Years of Psychotherapy,* 240.

[2] In fact, it was only in 1991, during Aristide's presidency that birth certificates issued to Haitians born in the rural areas no longer were officially titled (I should say branded) "peasant."

[3] "God is good. Whatever befalls us must be born gracefully and with patience. Such is life..." Thus, the Haitian countryman accepts his lot. Some development experts and many Westernized Haitians feel that this resigning of one's self to God's will, this religious attitude, is the stumbling-block to economic development since it discourages the necessary taking charge of one's head in the deliberate pursuit of one's own, capitalist self-interests.

[4] Haiti's very first constitution expressively forbade land ownership by whites and/or foreigners. The *Kreyòl blan* means both "white" and "foreigner." If you are a foreigner, you are a *blan* no matter what your color. There is, however, no xenophobia in Haiti.

[5] Unlike all later "revolutions" in the Third World, the Africans of Haiti were never part of a class struggle nor did they have a perspective of

history as dialectical materialism. Yet the way their society was organized, particularly regarding labor and the fruits of labor, gives one the sense that they were "Marxists" before Marx.

[6] Gerard Barthelemy. *Le Pays En Dehors: Essai sur l'Univers Rural Haitien*, 47. Editions Henri Deschamps/CIDICHA. Translation mine.

[7] *Ibid.*, 50.

[8] The Creole state has failed in Haiti as it has in Africa.

[9] In rural Haiti marriage is not the dominant form of union. More commonly found is the *plasaj* or co-habitation with one woman. This woman is known as *Madan Pyè* or *Madan Cherisme*—"Pierre's wife" or "Cherisme's wife"; never is she referred to by the man's surname. His *manman pitit*, the other women with whom he has children and that he takes care of, is considered literally "children's mother(s)."

[10] It is striking to notice that even if a Haitian countryman builds his house with straw, he will build his tombs in concrete. I believe there is a significant sociological statement made as to the importance attached to the dead. I am not convinced it is just an economic matter of not having enough money to build a house of concrete.

[11] Gathering usually early in the morning, sometimes before daybreak, men make their way to the garden of the *kombit's* organizer. Once there, work begins. Throughout the day, musicians, playing appropriate rhythms on the drums and horns, encourage the organizer and his companions to sing, joke, and banter, while working in unison. At noon, the women bring food and refreshment to the men. But their contribution is not restricted to just serving the men on their lunch break. They sometimes perform field work, too, particularly at harvest time. Money is rarely used. In exchange for their participation, the organizer feeds his helpers, provides the entertainment, and often distributes gallons of *kleren*, an alcohol made from fermented sugar cane juice. If and when monetary payment is made, the group usually chooses one member who is responsible for collecting and distributing the money. The organizer will be expected to participate in turn in the next *kombit* organized by one of the men who had helped him. And so it goes year round.

Women are an integral part of the Haitian economy in general, particularly in the rural areas' fields. They participate from the beginning to the end of the agricultural cycle. They play a prominent role in the "marketing" of the garden's products and are the primary economic agents of the rural world. It is one of the most typical "postcard" scenes of Haiti: countrywomen with 50-60 pound baskets of produce balanced on their heads, making their way down to the market from the neighboring hills. In town, they line the streets, side by side, selling the same things to passing buyers. Since there are no fixed prices for these products, every merchant is able to haggle with every customer until the best price is reached. The first sale of the day is not to just anyone though. The buyer has to show some "sympathy," some "positive vibration" toward the seller. How the first transaction is carried out is almost as important as the monetary value since that first sale is believed to have an effect on how well the rest of the sales go.

There are specific market days in the rural areas as well. Typically, sales occur under make shift tents erected in an open air space that developed into a market place, more by force of habit and convenience than by official urban planning. Women walking or riding down from all the adjacent areas will converge to that centralized area and spend the day haggling, buying, and selling. Afterwards, when there is either no buyer or nothing left to sell, they will all mount their mules or donkeys and head back to their homes.

[12] Its origin is source of scholarly debate. While some authors such as James Leyburn and Jules Faine see Creole as having been introduced to the Caribbean island by buccaneers speaking Norman with an additional sprinkling of Northern France's regional dialects, others, such as Pradel Pompilus, Suzanne Sylvain, Charles F. Pressoir accentuate the African influence on the language. It was not French and it was certainly not any one of the several languages and dialects spoken by the various ethnic groups thrown hodgepodge into the hellhole of colonial slavery. Developed during the past three hundred years, the language includes disparate elements of French, Spanish and English but with a grammatical structure more African than Latin. On the other hand, one might argue that *Kreyòl* is the most recent linguistic derivative of the latter as French, Spanish, Italian and Portuguese are all, practically speaking, *Kreyòls* of Latin.

[13] The use of the word "psychic" or "psychological" as an adjective presents a difficult choice: either we assume soul to be a working concept/symbol or we choose it to be "literally real"; in the first case we speak of the psycho-logical, in the second case of the psychic. I leave it to the reader to decide which of these attitudes fits his/her mode of "seeing" being human.

[14] Bruno Snell. *The Discovery of the Mind in Greek Philosophy and Literature*, 31.

[15] That aspect of *Vodu* is the one most sensationalized by Hollywood, particularly in movies of the Fifties. More recently, the movie made from Wade Davis' book *The Serpent and the Rainbow*, supposedly an ethnobotanists account of his search for the poison associated with the zombification

THE GARDEN AND THE GODS 79

process, did little more than thrill the fans of tall tales from the grave. The book, though, makes an earnest attempt at uncovering the mysteries played out in the *Vodu* rituals. Beyond the chemical connection, which certainly must satisfy the pure materialists among us, Davis does admit to magical operations being an integral, essential and definitive part of the complete zombification process.

[16] E.R. Dodds. *The Greeks and the Irrational*, 16.

[17] Bruno Snell.*Op. cit.*, 12.

[18] On page 381 in volume II of *Nations Nègres et Cultures*, C. Anta Diop refers to another author writing on the religion of the Yorubas. She says that in West Africa, the word which signifies "to exist" is *ye*. I am tempted to give the *Kreyòl ye* the same meaning because it is used specifically in that sense and no other. Yorubas were also brought to Haiti as slaves from Dahomey. Their rites, known in *Vodu* as *Ra-Da*, have been kept in almost pure form in a famous *lakou* called *Souvnans*, a name derived from a French word meaning "remembrance."

[19] There is also the expression *se menm noumenm lan* which translates as "it is we the same ourselves" used in situations such as when people fighting are being asked to "be reasonable": *pa goumen, se menm noumen lan,* "don't fight"...or when a newcomer, uncomfortable at meeting a group of people unknown to him but to whom he was sent by a mutual acquaintance, is told to relax and get comfortable: *mete-w alèz*...In both instances, the expression appeals to self-sameness as a means of bridging distance.

[20] C. G. Jung. *The Structure and Dynamic of the Psyche*, 17-18.

[21] The cultural differences explored here do seem to reflect specific functions associated with each hemisphere, as various experiments and studies have shown. Thus, the left brain manifests a mode of thinking known as analytical, linear, segregative, dia-bolic, "objective"; the right brain, on the other hand, perceives the similarity between things, is synthetic, congregative, sym-bolic, "subjective." In short, they overlap and function as a unified "field of consciousness." They may, if reinforced through culturally specific forms, reflect almost typical (in the Jungian sense) perceptions of a common "reality." No one will deny that while we today live on the same planet as did the humans before us, we do so in vastly different worlds. While these differences may be explained by "politics" or "economics," by "progress" or lack thereof, they may just as well be more appropriately explained by the workings of psyche.

[22] The origin of the word is variously interpreted. For Milo Rigaud, *vodu* is a compound of *vo* and *du*. In his book, *Secrets of Voodoo*, he says *vo* means "introspection" and *du* means "into the unknown." Alfred Métraux,

in his book, *Voodoo in Haiti*, says, "In Dahomey and Togo, among tribes belonging to the Fon language, a 'voodoo' is a 'god,' a 'spirit.'" As explained in *Nation Nègres et Cultures* by Cheik Anta Diop, the verb *vodu* means "to dress up" or cover one's self by wearing a "pagne" or short skirt. Although he doesn't use the word in reference to Haiti, I find that it applies well to the Haitian rites in that *vodu* alludes to the invisibility of the *lwa* discovered and hidden by the rituals. Heraclitus says, "The real constitution of each thing is accustomed to hide itself" (quoted by James Hillman in *Dream and the Underworld*, 26).

[23] A "nation," the exact meaning of *nanchon*, was "originally" the ensemble of all those born of the same ancestry, i.e., that possessed the same "nature" given by blood line or "linkage" to dead ancestors.

[24] I am not aware of any attempts at retracing the word *lwa* to its root. It might not have any, and simply be the *Kreyòl* spelling of the French *loi* as in *L'Esprit des Lois*, "The Spirit of the Laws" of Montesquieu, or as in *les lois de la Nature* (the laws of Nature). It would be the one key word by which we could begin to look at *Vodu* in a different light by demystifying it. It would then mean that the Africans thought that the loi(s) or lwa(s) of *Vodu* are laws of Nature and vice-versa. Since humans are born by Nature, live and die in it, it was tautological for ancient Africans and their descendants to "animate" everything as they felt animated by everything.

The meaning of the ancient Egyptian word *neter*, commonly translated as *god*, might have suffered the same fate as the word *lwa* though not in the literal but in the interpretive sense. To wit: In Vol I. of E. A. Wallis Budge's *The Gods of The Egyptians*, we find excerpts from other works by other writers of the same period. "The fundamental meaning of the word was 'the operative power which created and produced things by periodical recurrence, and gave them new life and restored to them the freshness of youth'"; "One knows not exactly the meaning of the verb *nuter*, which forms the radical of the word *nuter*, 'god.' It is an idea analogous to 'to become,' or 'renew oneself,' for *nuteri* is applied to the resuscitated soul which clothes itself in its immortal form"; "an Egyptian god is a being who is born and dies, like man, and is finite, imperfect, and corporeal, and is endowed with passions, and virtues, and vices." Budge himself says, "It is impossible not to think that the word has a meaning which is closely allied to the ideas of 'self-existence,' and the power 'to renew life indefinitely,' and 'self-production.' In other words *neter* appears to mean a being who has the power to generate life, and to maintain it when generated. It is useless to attempt to explain the word by Coptic etymologies, for it has passed over directly into the Coptic language under the form *nouti*, and *noute*, the last consonnant, *r*, having disappeared through phonetic decay, and the translators of the Holy Scriptures from that language used it to express the words 'God' and "Lord.'" It is not impossible that *neter*, taken as a linguistic archetype, relates phonetically and "spiritually" to *nature*, which is close to the Latin *natus*, and found in the French *naitre* (to be born), though I am not claiming that Latin derives from ancient Egyptian. It is ironic that Ancient Egyptians, having to be practical men on account of the fact that there were no precedents, saw the word "as is," in the strictest sense. They might have seen the laws of nature as active principles in creation and re-creation. Later Westerners came to name these laws "gods" and later still, "forces." Seeing and knowing Nature's wonders "scientifically" over thousands of years would not necessarily prevent Ancient Egyptians, these human pioneers, from celebrating the same mysteries psycho-logically in an artistic and humorous way. After all, these people ate their gods! For a full treatment of Ancient Egyptian as a mother-tongue, see Gerald Massey's *A Book of the Beginnings*, in two volumes, first published in London in 1881 and published in 1995 by Black Classic Press.

[25] E. A. Wallis Budge. *The Gods of the Egyptians—Studies in Egyptian Mythology.* Vol. I, 3.

[26] C. G. Jung. *The Structure and Dynamic of the Psyche*, 110.

[27] C. G. Jung. Op. cit., 412.

[28] Maya Deren. *Divine Horsemen: The Living Gods of Haiti*, 27.

[29] E. A. Wallis Budge. *Osiris and The Egyptian Resurrection*, 17.

[30] Harold Courlander. *The Drum and The Hoe: Life and Lore of the Haitian People*, 21.

[31] The *mambre* is the family's psychic inheritance complex. I would venture a guess and say that linguistically *manbre* is a French derivative phonetically close to *membre* which in French means "member" as in member of family or member of the body.

[32] Maya Deren. *Op. cit.*, 72.

[33] *Rogatwa*, the functional equivalent of an "altar," is one of those *Kreyòl* terms in which it is easy to recognize the French root. In this case, *rogatwa* is a shorter version of *interrogatoire*. The *interrogatoire* is a noun which is not an object nor a place but rather the asking of questions. Standing, kneeling or sitting in front of the *rogatwa*, the *sèvitè* talks to the Invisible Ones. He asks questions, supplicates, invocates and gives thanks. He complains of ill treatment by others, neglect on the part of the *granmoun yo* or elders, i.e., both the deceased relatives and the greater *Lwas* themselves. It is not unusual in Haiti to see and hear someone addressing the statue of a saint in public. It is not considered odd at all.

[34] James Hillman. *A Blue Fire: Selected Writings*, 56.

[35] Alfred Métraux. *Voodoo in Haiti*, 200.

[36] James Hillman. "How Jewish is Archetypal psychology?" *Spring 53*, 1992, 125.

[37] Harold Courlander. Op. cit., pg. 33.

[38] This might account for the lack of pretense, profound humility and courteous civility which is so characteristic of the personality of most Haitians living *andeyò*, as anyone familiar with that society will attest. Too often these remarkable traits are seen by the urbane as the marks of hillbillies (*neg mòn*), dim-witted dunces at best.

[39] Wallis Budge. *Osiris and the Egyptian Resurrection*, Vol. I, 258.

[40] Alfred Metraux. Op. cit., 257.

[41] James Hillman. Op. cit., 46.

[42] Maya Deren. Op. cit., 26-7.

[43] Ibid., 44.

[44] Wallis Budge. Op. cit., Introduction, lxiv.

[45] There is a passage on page 218 in Wade Davis' *The Serpent and the Rainbow* which illustrates the misapprehension in regards to both terms as well as the relationship that exists between the concepts themselves: "The two aspects of the *vodoun* soul, the *ti bon ange* and the *gros bon ange*, are best explained by a metaphor commonly used by the Haitians themselves. Sometimes when one stands in the late afternoon light the body casts a double shadow, a dark core and then a lighter penumbra, faint like the halo that sometimes surrounds the full moon. This ephemeral fringe is the *ti bon ange*—the little good angel—while the image at the center is the *gros bon ange*—the big good angel. The latter is the life force that all sentient beings share; it enters the individual at conception and functions only to keep the body alive. At clinical death, it returns immediately to God and once again becomes part of the great reservoir of energy that supports all life...the *ti bon ange* is the part of the soul directly associated with the individual." Whether Davis reverses the role of the two aspects of the soul or not is not important here. The metaphor which he relates provides the adequate image to grasp the interrelationship of both constituents.

[46] Victor White. *God and the Unconscious*, 126.

[47] Ean Begg, quoted by Stephan A. Hoeller. In *Jung and the Lost Gospels: Insights into the Dead Sea Scrolls and the Nag Hammadi Library*, 88.

[48] Stanislav Grof. *Beyond the Brain: Birth, Death and Transcendence in Psychotherapy*, 179.

[49] Stephan A. Hoeller. Op. cit., 126.

[50] Theodore Roszac. *Where the Wasteland Ends*, 224.

TEACHING HAITIAN VODOU

CLAUDINE MICHEL

An early Portuguese explorer reported after a visit to the southern coast of Africa that the people had no religion. According to one commentator,

> ...his mistake was understandable. After all, he was from Europe, where the presence of religion is manifested in church buildings, priests, and sacred scriptures...[In Africa] he saw no identifiable religious buildings, no distinctively religious functionaries, and certainly no scriptures. Therefore: [the statement] *"they have no religion."*[1]

African religions, and Vodou for that matter, are not necessarily recognizable as separate institutions with a book of law regimenting the moral life of its devotees. They pervade and permeate the whole society as their "theology, rituals and organizations intimately merged with the concepts and structure of secular institutions," a commentary originally made by Yang about China which, for similar reasons, has also been said to be *a country without religion.*[2]

Claudine Michel is Associate Professor of Black Studies, Univeristy of California, Santa Barbara. She is the author of *Aspects Moraux et Educatifs du Vodou Haitien* (1995) and co-author of *Théories du Developpment de l'Enfant, Etudes Comparatives* (1994) as well as many other articles about the Caribbean and Africa.

It is, however, important to note that Booth's statement does not take into account the separate order of religion found among some European lower classes. He refers here to the phenomenology of Christianity (megalithic cathedrals, clergy, etc.) launched by medieval ruling classes (imperial aristocracies, papal empowerment, bureaucratic hierarchies), who conceived religion as a cosmic totality. To the extent that this phenomenology is used to "represent" Western theocracy, it conceals the religious folkways of the lower classes (the social movements of heresy and evangelicals, for example) which resisted the appropriation of religion by the upper classes. Therefore, Vodou as well as other non-Western religions, are in opposition with the *church establishment*, not with Christian spirituality *per se*.

In Haiti, the ancestral religion is important not as a "separate institution," but because in its *diffused* form it performs a pervasive though organized function which regulates all aspects of the spiritual, social, and even economic and political life of Vodou adherents—an observation true also of other societies and religions outside the Western umbrella.[3]

Family Vodou

The country continues to be an overwhelmingly rural society and, as such, the cult of the ancestors is the guardian of peasant traditional values and is largely linked to rural family life and to matters of land. Haitian peasants *serve the spirits* daily in their home, on their land, as they work, and gather with members of their extended family and kin on special occasions for more elaborate ceremonies, which may range from the *birthday* of a *spirit* to a *"service"* for a particular event affecting the family or the land. In remote areas, people sometimes walk for days to partake in such ceremonies which may take place as often as several times a month, or as rarely as once or twice a year.

The Vodou religion is known to be closely tied not only to issues of division and administration of land but also to matters of economy as it relates to the residential areas, *the lakous*.⁴ It is concerned with conflict resolution and the overall well-being of its residents. This kind of *family* or *domestic* Vodou, practiced primarily within the context of the family network, is the type that the Haitian diaspora has taken with it overseas, using its African spirituality as frame of reference to help assure its collective survival in physical and social environments hostile, more often than not, to Haitian immigrants.

Throughout Haiti, in New York, in Paris, as in any other location where Vodou is practiced, the absence of a formal place of worship is noticeable. There is no Vodou church *per se*; instead, *all* places are sites of worships. The *hounfò*, the Vodou temple, is but one such place where the living gather to communicate with the spirits. It is usually (except if owned by an extremely rich family or by government officials) a very informal place, made of very simple material, not completely enclosed, with sometimes a dirt floor, and having no furniture (except for maybe a few chairs and drums, some flags, and pictures). The *hounfò* is quite different from typical places of worship related to other religions. In fact, it may not be readily identified as such, even during a ceremony, which an uniformed observer might mistakenly take for a social gathering with no specific goal.

In the Vodou world, among other sites, the cemetery as well as the *crossroads* are prominent and meaningful places of worship; the cemetery as repository of spirits and the crossroads, as points of access to the world of the invisible—the point where the mortal world crosses the metaphysical plane. Oceans, rivers, and chutes also have special significance in Vodou because important and demanding spirits, such as *Simbi, Agwe, Maitresse dlo*, or *La Sirène* (the mermaid), reside in those large bodies of water. It is also believed that water has special powers, and that, for example, some individuals are initiated *anba dlo*, or under water.⁵

Other places of remarkable religious importance include: various sites of pilgrimage, the parish church, as well as the fields, the markets, the compounds and households. Often, in a Vodou home the only recognizable religious items are some images of saints and a few candles with a rosary; in other homes, where people may more openly show their devotion to the *spirits,* noticeable items may include: an altar with Catholic deities and iconographies, rosaries, bottles, jars and rattles decorated or not, perfumes, oils, dolls, rags and a few other paraphernalia. This systematic absence of readily identifiable religious objects in "specifically designated sacred locations" is understandable for two reasons: (1) Vodou's continuous presence in all aspects of Haitian life and its overarching influence; (2) the fact that for so long Haitians had to practice their religion clandestinely. The lack of formal settings of worship reflects both the persistence and adaptiveness of the Haitian religion.

Temple Vodou

Vodou in the more densely populated urban areas has been called "temple Vodou" where communal life revolves around the *hounfòs* and the head of the temples, the *manbos* and *houngans*, respectively priestesses and priests in the Vodou religion. Though, in most cases, few distinguishing marks identify these sites as places of worship, they remain the center of life in the cities. Through them, the devotees recreate the family and kin lost when they migrated to the city and continue their quest for religious and moral values. Vodou temples are often located near churches, yet another element of spatial juxtaposition of Haiti's complex religious traditions. It is not unusual, for example, for people to leave a Vodou ceremony early in the morning and to step right into the four o'clock Mass at a nearby Catholic church. In addition to the complex cosmological reasons behind such behavior, to be seen in church was traditionally a form of self-protection against possible persecutions and gossips. To be a faithful churchgoer is perceived as a sign of being a "good" Christian—someone who honors God and the saints, and who therefore, enjoys the respect of the Vodou community.

Although temples are mostly an urban phenomenon, this does not mean that *hounfòs* are not found in rural areas; neither does this mean that urbanites have abandoned domestic worshipping. Mostly, temple communities have common characteristics with the family cult though they sometimes exhibit differences, in particular in the areas of division of labor, spectators *v.* performers and greater hierarchization more visible in the temples than in families. Myths and rituals may differ from one *hounfò* to another, from one Vodou family to another, depending on the region, on the types of spirits who are served and invoked, on the style of worship chosen by a particular family, or on the specific issues facing a given community. However, they should mostly be viewed from the perspective of their commonness.

In the Vodou world where so many elements merge to form a diversified but always coherent whole, places of worship are not mutually exclusive, compartmentalized and categorized. Their functionality is what matters. This utilitarian characteristic is also what partly[6] explains the nonexistence of written dogma and the absence of specific instructional material in a context where teaching takes place *everywhere* and where *everything* represents an opportunity for growth and learning. More simply, Haitians have not developed written dogma and instructional material for the same reason that they have not built ostensibly recognizable and elaborate temples: they do not need them because they have no use for them. The proverb says, "Where there is a need, there is a way." In this particular instance, "There is no *way* because there is no *need.*"

Characteristics of Teachers and Learners

Like everything else in Vodou, the issue of teachers and learners is quite complex. In Vodou society everyone continually plays the role of teacher and learner in a process of continuing exchanges and dialogues during on-going interactions with family members, the community and the spirits. Elders, parents, members of the extended family, neighbors, priests and priestesses most often play the role of teachers and guides for the younger generations though they can also, at times, turn into learners among their peers and *vis-a-vis* the spirits. Senior members of the community may become learners, for example, in a situation where a young child may carry a message from an elder or from one of the spirits.

To be a good teacher one has to respect the *flow of nature,* Vodou's non-hierarchization as well as its functionality—all things that the learner also ought to master. Teachers and learners, in many ways, have the same agenda; they may just achieve these goals differently and at different moments of their human journey. Courlander wrote about Vodou's flexibility and limited directiveness:

> Vodou permeates the land, and, in a sense, it springs from the land. It is not a system imposed from above, but one which pushes out from below. It is a thing of the family, a rich and complex inheritance from a man's own ancestors. It is not the priests of Vodoun who control and direct its course. They, like the lowest peasant simply move about within it and make use of its resources.[7]

For those who serve the spirits, life is about movement between people, movement between the living and the departed, and Vodou teaching and learning entail balancing commonalities and differences to create global harmony and peace. "Movement" refers here to sets of complex "interactions" among people, among people and the spirits, and reflects the different roles and functions involved in these rapports. In Haitian Creole, "balans" or "balanse" means to bring about equilibrium, to harmonize; it implies metaphysical elements not rendered by the English word "balance." These concepts also denote that teachers and learners play equally active roles in learning and teaching about the fluidity of the Vodou world and its ever-evolving cosmology. In that respect, Vodou's teaching approach is, in many ways, "learner-centered" with "teachers" serving primarily as guides and facilitators. This democratic foundation makes Vodou quite a progressive system compared to other more doctrinal world religions.

The Teachers—those who have "konesans"

Everyone who has *konesans*[8] is typically a Vodou teacher, that is, a person who continuously participates in the propagation of the Vodou worldview and assists in clarifying choices for less experienced individuals. However, the "better" teachers perform in addition more complicated tasks. Seniority, experience, wisdom, accompanied with *konesans*, and always coupled with style, characterize these more effective teachers. They are truly skilled at helping others *balanse* their lives within the web of relationships of their community and deal with both symptomatic and asymptomatic disturbances of nature's harmony which they help restore. All Vodou adepts can be teachers, but clearly *houngans* and *manbos* hold specially designated teaching roles in the Haitian communities where they engage in sophisticated ministration and healing.

Though they do not wear a recognizable garb and do not attend formal theological centers for their training, these priests and priestesses are well-respected and powerful members of society. Having undergone the fourth and highest level of initiation which confirmed them as priests or priestesses and healers, *houngans* and *manbos* have leverage in the world of the spirits, a status which does not make them leaders in the most commonly used sense of the term but, one which allows them to "lead" their community.[9] In Vodou, the good leaders follow; the good teachers listen in order to "see things clearly" and help participants choose wisely among different possible paths. The functions that they perform are essential to the communal well-being: they minister, preside, heal, see and foresee. In other words, they restore equilibrium and keep things balanced through various forms of ritualizing and rituals. The skilled ritualizer—someone who knows how to orchestrate the arrival of the spirits and solicit their intervention in human affairs—is therefore a powerful technician of the sacred, a true moral leader and a teacher of distinction.

Furthermore, to the extent that some form of morals and ethics constitutes the essence of all religions, the life of the *houngans* and *manbos*, their deeds and tenets—as individuals and as people who orchestrate religious gatherings for the benefit of their Vodou family—tend to reflect the moral beliefs of those who serve the spirits. What emerges from their lives and ministrations represents a repository of *konesans*, of wisdom, and experience. They are teachers *par excellence*, not because they are necessarily moral exemplars, but because with the assistance of the spirits, they help the community find cohesion and teach Vodou adepts how to avoid the source of moral decay, imbalance. McCarthy Brown, explaining that in Vodou, the moral problem is not evil but imbalance, writes about the role of the moral leader:

> In the context of this pluralistic and conflict-centered description of life, the moral leader is not one who sets his or her own life up as a model of imitation. It is rather that person who, as a subtle and skilled technician of the sacred, can orchestrate ritual contexts in which each person discovers how to dance his or her own way through a process of dynamic balancing with others who dance in their own way.[10]

Most Vodou teachers officiate exclusively in their own communities whereas some of the more accomplished ones extend their ministrations further than their immediate world, accepting outsiders and sometimes foreigners into their Vodou family. Two such examples are Mathilda Beauvoir who officiates in Paris and Mama Lola, a renowned Vodou priestess who resides in Brooklyn; both have foreigners "eating at her table."[11] Though this may not be the rule, other cosmopolitan Vodou practitioners believe like them, that race, color, or nationality should never be factors in making the decision to include or not a person in Vodou ritualizing or in a Vodou family. Mama Lola, for example, trusts that it is not for us to decide who the spirits call.[12]

Also, many famous Haitian painters and artists are Vodou initiates if not *houngans*[13] and, as such, they are important Vodou teachers in both the local context and in the international community. Through their paintings or iron cast work, they teach about

Black aesthetics, the Haitian world and the Vodou worldview. The *Vodou Soul* and the *Haitian Spirit* are expressed in rather powerful ways in these pieces of artwork where signs and shapes become a message with a life of their own.

The *loas* and ancestral spirits are the other weighty Vodou teachers who harmonize specific aspects of life and serve as intermediaries between the humans and the ultimate self-existent *Bondye*, the *Grand Mèt*, the absolute and supreme Being, a concept which "shares much in common with Christian understandings of the deity."[14] To that effect, Mbiti wrote: "The God described in the Bible is none other than the God who is already known in the framework of traditional African religiosity."[15] In other words, there is a distinct monotheism in Vodou despite its henotheism and its pantheon of divinities and ancestral spirits. However, God, is not the usual focus of worship in a Vodou service; people typically pray *Bondye* through the mediation of the spirits. In turn, *Bondye* does not get involved directly in the devotees' daily existence and in their personal relations with the spirits. Paris comments: "The deity's remoteness does not evidence any lack of concern for humanity. It rather connotes the reverse. By maintaining distance from nature and humanity the deity manifests divine care,"[16] although not in a direct tangible fashion like the other Vodou teachers. Zuesse offers an interesting summation of this African perspective which also applies to the Haitian experience:

> It is an expression of his continuing benevolence that [God] has withdrawn his overwhelming power and presence behind the intermediary beings he has appointed to govern the modulated realm of specific beings. God does not get involved himself too directly in the world that he sustains, for too particular and intense involvement might destroy the fabric of the divine order he sustains.[17]

Though Zuesse uses "he" to refer to the Supreme Deity it is, however, not absolutely clear that the Haitian concept of God is altogether masculine in that the Vodou religion thrives to create harmony and maintain equilibrium, among other aspects, in the area of gender. Female and male spirits are, therefore, invoked frequently and served with equal deference, each one presiding over a specific, often "gendered" realm of human affairs. The power of the female *loas* represents an important lesson in itself, particularly for Haitian women who have endured such a long history of political and domestic oppression. In Vodou, women are priestesses, revered spirits, and fully participating members of their religious communities which offers one of their rare sources of hope for a more egalitarian society. In this respect, the Haitian ancestral cult empowers women more than most other world religions.

The spirits most often served, and consequently, some of Vodou's most prominent teachers, include: *Dambala*, supreme, oldest, most respected, represented by a snake; *Aida Wedo*, his wife; *Legba*, the spirit of the crossroads who must be invoked to "open the gate" for the other *loas*; *Ogou* who does not tolerate injustice and who controls power; *Erzili*, representing sexuality, lesbianism, motherhood; *Azaka*, the peasant, the worker, the one who controls money; *Baron Samedi* and *Gran Brigit*, guardians of the cemeteries; *Gédé*, the spirit of death and sexuality. Most of these divinities exhibit various personalities and characteristics depending on the names that they take. For example, *Ogou Badagri* behaves quite differently from *Ogou Ferraille*, *Erzili Freda* from *Erzili Jérouge*, *Gédé Nimbo* from *Gédé Loray*, although the family relationship remains.

Each *loa* is an archetype of a moral principle that he or she represents although: "Virtue for both the *loa* and those who serve them is less an inherent character trait than a dynamic state of being that demands ongoing attention and care."[18] Like humans, they are whole, with strengths and weaknesses. McCarthy Brown says it well:

> Vodou spirits are larger than life but not other than life." She further comments: "The spirits talk with the faithful. They hug them, hold them, feed them, but also chastise them…The Vodou spirits are

not models of the well-lived life; rather, they mirror the full range of possibilities inherent in the particular slice of life over which they preside. Failure to understand this has led observers to portray the Vodou spirits as demonic or even to conclude that Vodou is a religion without morality—a serious misconception.[19]

Moreover, from Vodou's holistic conception of life derives the fundamental idea that the Vodou spirits are not saints because they are good but because they are all-encompassing, global, full, complex, and because, as such, they mirror human life, its poles and conflicts. Though these conflicts are manifestations of existing contradictions and of disturbances in the web of human relations, "the point is not to make conflict go away, but to make it work for, rather than against life."[20]

The Vodou spirits of the Haitian pantheon are teachers of distinction not because they guide by rigid examples or indoctrination but because they heighten the worshippers' vision of the world that they live in. *Loas* do not preach, nor do they typically advice *per se*. Through possession-performances, they help participants explore potentialities and choices by highlighting destructive and constructive aspects of particular situations. At times, they may appear disorganized, unfocused because they find it necessary to throw people off balance in order to help them find balance. They are, however, rarely off target: they always know what the issues are (sometimes, before the parties involved) and ceaselessly succeed in clarifying matters for the participants, helping them see what they may sometimes be oblivious to in their lives. The *loas* usually do not introduce what is not already there; their task is to show devotees how to see clearly in the midst of a multiplicity of truths.

The Learners—the entire Haitian community

From its youngest members to its most acclaimed technicians of the sacred, all are lifelong learners in the Vodou faith. Adepts of the Haitian religious community continuously struggle to balance their lives in order to learn how to follow a moral path, ever guided by the overarching African ethos on which their religion is based. A "good" learner makes appropriate efforts according to age and status to incorporate the spirit of Vodou and its worldview in a relevant, lively and harmonized existence during which unrelenting, interconnected and responsible relationships are maintained for the benefit of the group.

Young children and youth are exposed to learning which involves mostly copying and imitating adults and elders. This informal type of education continues until children, youth and young adults become socialized into their society, until behavior and rituals have become habitual, until they have incorporated the traditional values of their culture into an harmonious blend of secular and religious activities. The very participation in the "regular" life of a Vodou family fosters this kind of informal learning and creates opportunities for informal education to occur, as with all other forms of Vodou teaching, outside the Haitian school system. Informal education is, in this case, the more deliberate and systematic ways used by servitors of the spirits, in particular those who have *konesans* to teach pre-planned curricular items to those coming of age and those wishing to become "formally" initiated in Vodou.

The four levels of Vodou initiation (the specific steps taken to confer "ascending degrees of control" to humans in their relationships with the spirits), with the highest of these levels being the actual rising to the status of priesthood, fit, for example, into this category of informal education. Specific training is also undergone by other functionaries of a *hounfò*, such as, for example, the *Laplace* and the *Hounsis* who go through a long and formal apprenticeship with the head of the temples. Sustained and organized efforts are made during each stage of initiation to teach about particular rituals and reinforce character. Initiation is a complex, sophisticated, highly ritualistic and, sometimes, costly process.[21] Dunham made those revelations:

We began the ritual of the crossed and recrossed handclasp, the bow with knees flexed, turn underarm, [those] of highest protocol guiding the other. Then, the turn to all four directions of the compass, hand gripped tightly in hand, with sacred words spoken in each direction, the approach to the altar, the recognition of each grade of protocol by obeisance and work...It was up to my instructors to decide what to do, and I followed them, asking no questions...We danced, not as people in the houngfor, with the stress of possession or the escapism of hypnosis or for catharsis, but as I imagine dance when it must have been executed when body and being were more united, when form and flow and personal ecstasy became an exaltation of a superior state of things, not necessarily a ritual to any one superior being.[22]

Vodou cosmology emphasizes uniformity, conformity, group cohesion, support for one another. Initiation ceremonies are a primary conveyor of this worldview and initiates are rid of their will and desire to impose their ego on others. McCarthy Brown explains that it is "a spirituality that is more about empowerment than about gaining power over others."[23] During initiation, the neophytes are taught to liberate themselves from obstacles that may hinder their spiritual development: individuality, self-love, doubt, fears. During the days of seclusion, they become one with all other living creatures as well as with the four main forces of nature (air, fire, water, and earth). To be initiated, to *kouche* (literally to lie down), represents, in the most simplistic term, the death of the old self, and the birth of a new self, originating from a type of non-individualistic collective consciousness. One is forced to regress into infancy and childhood—and, consequently, is treated as it is appropriate for these stages—only to be brought back, through rituals designed to overcome fear, pain, and selfishness, to a new state of adulthood and maturity. An initiate explains some of the feelings accompanying the initiation process:

> It was hard to become a child again, to let go of being in charge of myself, to give the care of myself over to another. Most diffi-

cult was letting go of words, of the appearance of control...I bit my tongue to stop the *How? and When? and Why?*...Entering the chamber was like dying...The drums were pounding as they had been for hours...Seven times I raised my hand and then darkness...I was thrown off-balance in order to learn to find balance...Ever so briefly I died...[24]

When the initiates leave the chamber where they are secluded, their heads are covered. It must remain so for forty days after initiation.[25] Clearly, the How, the exercise of the art of initiation, represents a moral message in itself: the forces of life and death are reckoned with, the limits of knowledge and power are challenged, truth and faith are revalorized through the initiation process—all this being, at the very least, an experience in humility and brotherhood.

All learn about Vodou starting from an early age in their home, in their extended family, in their community while attending Vodou ceremonies or participating in services at home or in a *hounfò*. However, with age comes not only increased privileges but additional responsibilities. The youth are expected to participate more and more in Vodou rituals, to guide younger children, to show increased respect for elders, to develop their sense of humanism and to learn to emphasize the common good over individual satisfactions. In order words, they are expected to systematically incorporate the Haitian secular and religious beliefs in a sustained effort to live a relevant and moral existence and to maintain equilibrium within their community.

However, as in other educational arenas, some learners are more perceptive and more talented than others. The good learner is a person who is receptive to the message communicated by the spirits, the elders, or even the group of peers, someone who is attentive to the aesthetic guiding every endeavor and encounter. The proficient learner is thus skilled at orchestrating the "reception of messages" and pays attention not only to content but also style, always striving to stay in touch with both the inner self and the outside world. The accomplished learner is open, honest, observant, vigilant, unblocked, extended; he or she is mindful of the traditions and values being passed down and loyal to the messages of the cosmic world.

Moreover, the consummated learner is often also a good *chwal* for the *loas*, that is, someone who easily and skillfully receives the spirits and their messages through possession or in their dreams. Someone who has been possessed by a god is said to be the *chwal*, the horse of the *loa*, someone whose *gro bonanj* (guardian angel/spirit/soul) has been displaced by that of the spirit who mounted her. The person possessed is in a state of trance. She is not conscious and is no longer herself but the incarnation of the *loa*. In particular, this is an area where *manbos* and *houngans* excel as students of the spirits and of the ancestors, making it possible for the gods to enter their bodies, becoming, by extension, gods themselves through spiritual and charnel communion.

The propagation of moral principles and educational values assumes many forms in Vodou communities. It happens during ceremonies, while interacting with the spirits or with other Vodou participants; in the homes and outside, while fulfilling one's daily activities around family members and in the larger community. In other words, one learns everywhere and at all times. More than actual "moral" principles, what is communicated inside and outside Vodou families is a worldview, a particular sensitivity and perspective on life — the *Vodou ethos* formed and informed by both African cosmological understandings and American and Creole realities.

Notes

[1] Newell S. Booth, Jr., ed. "An Approach to African Religion" in *African Religions: A Symposium*. New York: Nok Publishers, 1977, 1.

[2] Ch'ing- Kum Yang. *Religion in Chinese Society: A Study of Contemporary Social Functions of Religions and Some Historical Factors*. Berkeley, CA: University of California Press, 1970, 20.

[3] *Ibid*. Yang made, for example, similar remarks about China. So did Booth: "There are interesting affinities between African and Chinese traditional religion." "An Approach to African Religion," 10.

⁴ Literally *lakou* means "yard." The word *lakou* evokes the idea of many large extended families sharing a common compound and yard. It represents a residual structure of the African village.

⁵ *Anba dlo* literally means under water. Haitians believe that some people spend time "under water," down in *Ginen* (a Haitian appellation for Africa) as part of their initiation as priests and priestesses. This "inexpensive" type of initiation, unlike the more formal ones which may be somewhat costly, are considered a special "gift." Mathilda Beauvoir, who officiates primarily in Paris, may well be the most renowned *anba dlo* initiate. Also see: Harold Courlander. *The Drum and the Hoe*. Berkeley, CA: University of California Press, 1973, 19.

⁶ Other reasons include by order of importance (1) the essence of the Vodou worldview itself, (2) the orality which characterizes Haitian culture, (3) until recently, the lack of a standardized Creole spelling, (4) the unavailability of writers to produce such documents, (5) a clear lack of funding and resources to engage in such an activity.

⁷ Harold Courlander. *Haiti Singing*. New York: Cooper Square Pub, 1973, 7.

⁸ *Konesans* means knowledge, but the Creole word is stronger than its English counterpart in that it encompasses the notions of experience mixed with wisdom, usually acquired with age. Typically, elders, houngans and manbos, the departed, the ancestors have a lot of *konesans*.

⁹ Especially during the Duvalier era, many such religious "leaders" were also members of the government.

¹⁰ Karen McCarthy Brown. "Alourdes: A Case Study of Moral Leadership in Haitian Vodou," in *Saints and Virtues*, J.S. Hawley, ed. Berkeley, CA: University of California Press, 1987, 167.

¹¹ In Haiti, eating is a life-sustaining activity in more ways than one. It is a means of maintaining ties; to say that someone eats at one's table or at one's place is a way of expressing the closeness of a relationship.

¹² See: Kathy McCarthy Brown. *Mama Lola; A Vodou Priestess in Brooklyn*. Berkeley, CA: University of California Press, 1991. Mama Lola's reputation goes further than the boundaries of the Haitian community. Though many other technicians of the Vodou religion share her worldly approach, the international impact of her ministrations remains unusual.

¹³ Here I specifically refer to *houngans* and not *manbos*. Though Vodou is not a religion which differentiates between gender, there are still very few internationally renowned female painters and artists.

¹⁴ Peter Paris. *The Spirituality of African Peoples, The Search for a Common Moral Discourse*. Minneapolis: Fortress Press, 1995, 29.

¹⁵ *Ibid*. John Mibiti in *The Spirituality of African People*, 29.

¹⁶ *Ibid*., 30.

¹⁷ *Ibid*., 31.

¹⁸ McCarthy Brown, *Mama Lola*, 6.

¹⁹ *Ibid*.

²⁰ McCarthy Brown, "Alourdes: A Case Study", 166.

[21] For more details on Vodou initiation, see McCarthy Brown, "Plenty Confidence in Myself: The Initiation of a White Woman Scholar into Haitian Vodou" *Journal of Feminist Studies in Religion*, vol. 3, no. 1 (Spring 1987), 67-76; also, Katherine Dunham, *Island Possessed*. Chicago: The University of Chicago Press, 1969, reprinted 1994.

[22] Dunham, *Island Possessed*, 108-109.

[23] McCarthy Brown, "Plenty Confidence," 75.

[24] *Ibid.*, 73-75; McCarthy Brown wrote that although one is not allowed to reveal the secrets of Vodou initiation, she was permitted to write about her reactions such must be protected to the process. She cautioned, however, not to "over-interpret" her "metaphoric speech."

[25] Like a baby's skull, the new head, the new self, is believed to be vulnerable and as such must be protected.

The Sibyls:
Bridging Personal Identity
and Oracular Knowing

DIANNE SKAFTE

Who were the sibyls and how did they deliver their legendary oracles? This question has kindled the imagination of artists and writers for many centuries. The sibyl has been clothed in images ranging from a hapless girl who loses her wits, to a shrouded crone who toys with kings. I find the sibyls worthy of attention because they speak to a special place in psychological life. They were renowned for their ability to enter expanded states of consciousness while staying anchored in ego-awareness. Sibyls are the original "medial women" (to use Toni Wolff's term). They remind us that we can surrender to numinous sources of guidance beyond the personal self without feeling obliterated. Anyone who works with dreams, images, divination, or other imaginal realities can find inspiration in sibylline lore.

Before exploring these ideas further, we must look briefly at the sibyl's journey through Western history. I will refer to her

---

Dianne Skafte, Ph.D., is the Academic Vice President of Pacifica Graduate Institute in Santa Barbara, California. Her forthcoming book, *When Oracles Speak*, will be released by Harper San Francisco in October, 1997.

personage in both the singular and plural forms, for her identity divided and recombined many times across the ages. As we will see, the way a culture treats its sibylline women reveals a great deal about its attitude towards the intuitive, mytho-poetic function of the psyche. (Our own era has not scored very well on this measure.)

The first woman to be called "Sibylla" probably lived sometime during the seventh century B.C.E. in ancient Asia Minor, a location well known for its tradition of ecstatic prophecy and divination. Her name may have derived from words signifying "one who utters divine counsel." Scholars find it plausible that the original Sibylla was an actual individual who gained distinction for her astonishing oracles. Her name later became attached to an ongoing tradition of sacred verse which predicted the fate of cities and nations.[1]

Not given to gentle words, Sibylla often shocked her listeners by condemning their complacency and crudeness. She upbraided the Persians with these words: "Miserable fools! Why do you chase after everything unholy?" And she reminded all mortals that, "You are made of flesh. Someday you will be nothing. How can you pump yourselves up with no thought to the end of life?" The sibyl also warned nations of future wars, famine, disease, and natural disasters. Certain prophecies offered hope, however. One of the earliest sibylline oracles on record comforts the Greeks with these words: "You will fall into deep waters, but like a leather bottle you will never sink."[2]

The sibyl's verses were gathered into a series of books and circulated throughout the Greek world. Whenever a province was threatened or a strange event occurred, citizens hurriedly opened their collection of oracles and sought "counsel from the divine." For example, if stones rained from the sky, if a hermaphrodite were born, or if lightning struck a public building, it was felt that Divine Intentionality was making itself known. Reading the sacred oracles lent spiritual meaning to events and provided guidance for future action.

Early legends recounted that the sibyl's mother was an immortal nymph of the springs. The gift of oracular speech derived from her kinship with sacred waters issuing from the all-knowing Underworld. The prophetess's father, a human being, bequeathed to her the ability to see piercingly into the affairs of nations. But the combination of clairvoyance and political awareness must have been a heavy burden to carry. Heraclitus noted that the sibyl uttered her prophecies through unsmiling lips.

Poised between the mortal and immortal worlds, Sibylla was able to extend her life-span far beyond that of ordinary mortals. It was commonly believed that she lived to the age of 1000 years. To hold such a long tenure on earth inflamed the admiration of her followers, for everything ancient was highly venerated in the classical world.

One glimpse of the sibyl in her old age is found in a legend reported by Roman historians. During the reign of Tarquinius Superbus (534-510 B.C.E.) an exceedingly old woman appeared before the ruler. She displayed nine manuscript scrolls and offered to sell them for a colossal sum of money. "What books are these that ask such a ludicrous price?" Tarquinius scoffed. "The oracles of Sibylla," she answered. With an impatient gesture, the ruler told her to go away. The old woman then knelt down and ignited a small fire in front of Tarquinius. She calmly burned three of the rolls to ashes. "Now I have six books to offer you at the same price," she said. "Will you take them?" Tarquinius did not know whether to laugh or explode into rage. "Be gone with you!" he shouted. The crone knelt down again and placed three more rolls into the flames. "I offer you the remaining oracles for the same price," she said.

Tarquinius suddenly felt uneasy. He sent for his augers (who received oracular communications from birds) and asked them what he should do. When the augers heard about the scrolls, they gasped, for their signs had predicted a god-sent blessing would be offered to the state. If the blessing were rejected, great misfortune would befall. "Buy the scrolls at all costs!" they urged. Tarquinius hastily paid the woman what she asked. She then walked away and was never seen again. It is said that the good fortune deriving from these books lasted throughout the whole history of the state, and that many disasters were averted because of the sibyl's remarkable prophecies.[3]

The story of Tarquinius and the old sibyl spread throughout the Roman world. It illuminated the wondrous origins of those sibylline oracles kept safeguarded in the capitol. A spiritual lesson also could be gleaned from the tale: messages issuing from a divine source have value beyond reckoning. Sometimes they arrive by way of strange carriers, and sometimes we are asked to pay a price that seems high. But their blessings last a lifetime.

What was the sibyl's own experience of oracular inspiration? We can only speculate upon its nature from the fragments and clues which history has provided us. The sibyl appeared to work cojointly with her source of oracular knowing. When two things conjoin they do not merge; but neither do they remain entirely separate. In one oracle Sibylla says, "The great Divine commands me to prophesy all these things, and my words are not imperfect, nor in vain, once they are put into my mind."[4] We note that the Divine "commands" her to prophesy, and words are put into her mind. But her mouth is not taken over by the command. Sibylla refers to the prophecy as "my words," even though she experiences the communications as being given to her from a supernal source. In the relationship she describes, both her ego-consciousness and the source of inspired knowledge seem to find equal footing.

We may better understand the nature of sibylline prophecy by contrasting it with the work of other types of oracle-speaker from antiquity. The priestess of Delphi (also called the Pythoness or Pythia), cultivated the skill of mediumship. She was a woman of mid-life age, selected for her impeccable character and spiritual sensitivity. Leaving secular life behind, the priestess lived on the temple grounds and devoted herself to praying, fasting, and enacting sacred rituals. On appointed days of the year, she was escorted to the sacred seat of inspiration in the temple. Laurel branches (emblems of Apollo) were then placed into her hand. When the leaves began to tremble, everyone knew that the priestess had descended into the state of divine inspiration. The petitioner, who waited behind a curtain or wall, had submitted a question to temple officials in advance. After it was read aloud, the Pythoness offered an answer. It was assumed that Apollo himself was the power who spoke through the priestess's lips.

Sibylla, in contrast, belonged to no official establishment. Independence was her trademark, and she freely blasted the most powerful states on earth if the spirit so moved her. One could not petition the sibyl for oracles. She spoke prophecies according to her own inner prompting, and the affairs of individuals held little interest for her. Nearly all of her oracles addressed larger collective issues such as earth changes, war and peace, health and disease, and spiritual integrity. The sibyl would never have consented to submerge her personhood and become a mere channel for Apollo. She spoke on her own authority as a half-divine being, with long earthly experience to back her words.

Though impromptu, the sibyl's communications patterned themselves into hexameter verse, the meter of ancient Greek epic and didactic poetry. These verses were sung rather than spoken. The aesthetic quality of Sibylla's art hints at the deep connection between oracular knowing and creative inspiration. In many mythological traditions around the world we find that oracular communications are linked with the arts. Both modes of creation require us to draw upon sources of inspiration beyond the personal self, to foster non-linear ways of thinking, and to embrace mytho-poetic modes of expression.

Plutarch, writing in the first century of the common era, recalled an old legend in which the first sibyl on earth was taught to sing her verses by the Muses themselves. His image opens up a new way of understanding sibylline oracles. Perhaps her stark warnings to humankind were prompted not by anger but by a violated sense of beauty. Perhaps the sibyl's deepest intention was to help restore the aesthetic and spiritual foundations of community life.

THE SIBYLS

An Image Refracted

By late Roman times, the sibyl's identity had refracted into multiple images. Various sets of oracles now became associated with the Sibyls of Cumae, Erythrea, Tiburtina, Libya, Persia, Samos, and many others. Sibylla's breakup into satellite figures was accelerated by the fire of 83 B.C.E. which burned Rome's capitol and incinerated the original oracle scrolls bought by Tarquinius. Horrified at their loss, officials sent scouts into neighboring provinces to round up any records they could find of sibylline oracles. The resulting collection, known as the *Libri Sibyllini* was a hodgepodge of sayings, many of them scrawled in ungainly verse. Four centuries later, the *Libri Sibyllini* was ordered destroyed by a Christian general named Stilicho. Only a few fragments of the original oracle collections have survived into modern times.

But a more profound change was creeping over the sibyl's image. She was still honored as a source of prophecy, but her art now carried a tragic, tormented look. An example of this decline may be found in Virgil's depiction of a sibylline prophecy session, which is quite different from anything found in early Greek lore. Its details are worth reviewing, for they hint at the deteriorating state of oracular practice in the pagan world.

In chapter six of the *Aeneid*, we find Aeneas and his Trojan fleet landing on the coast of Cumae in ancient Italy. They desire to seek counsel with the famous sibyl who delivers oracles from the recesses of a vast cavern. After sacrificing seven steers to the deities, Aeneas and his men peer into the cave's mouth and await the prophetess. What they see sends a chill shuddering through their bones. Standing in the hollow, the priestess calls upon the Fates to inspire her with oracles. Then suddenly she turns pale and cries, "Behold the god! The god!" Now her hair flies into disarray and her breast heaves like a wild animal. The god is closing in. Virgil describes what happens next:

> She rages, savage, in her cavern, tries
> to drive the great god from her breast. So much

> the more, he tires out her raving mouth;
> he tames her wild heart, shapes by crushing force.
> And now the hundred great gates of the house [cave]
> swing open of their own accord. They bear
> the answers of the priestess through the air.[5]

Under the spell of prophetic fervor, the sibyl reveals all that she sees ahead—terrible wars, rivers foaming with blood, and a close comrade of Aeneas descending to the underworld in death. These are the hard oracles that come roaring from the sibyl's lips as Apollo "urges the reins" and "plies the spurs beneath her breast."

Aeneas receives these terrible predictions calmly. He can bear anything, he says, if only he may gaze upon the face of his departed father one more time. The sibyl grants his wish. She provides instructions on how to penetrate the fathomless underworld with the help of a magical golden bough.

Virgil's creative imagination fashioned a priestess who combined features of sibylline prophecy with features of Delphic practice. The ancient shamanic skill of guiding souls to the underworld also found its way into the scene. Virgil's synthesis of these traits is understandable, for many oracular traditions had melded together by the first century B.C.E.

What I find unsettling about this scene is the way Virgil portrays the sibyl's prophetic experience. Her relationship with oracular knowing is fitful, violent, cruel. Apollo (the source of illumination) heaps more abuse than inspiration upon his faithful priestess. He thrusts spurs in her breast, drives her with reins, crushes her heart, and finally tires out her mouth before she submits to his will. These images may speak to the pagan world's increasing fear and distrust of oracular art, as well as the devalued position of women.

The poet Lucan, writing a century after Virgil, painted his prophetess in even less happy colors. In *Pharsalia*, Lucan tells us how the warrior Appius visits the almost-defunct Delphic shrine to seek an oracle. The priestess who resides there does not want to go into the sacred sanctuary, for Apollo fills her heart with dread.

But a temple official hurls it across the threshold.

Overcome by divine power, the priestess dashes around the cave like a mad Bacchant, knocking over the sacred tripod from where oracles once were delivered. Her hair bristles, her body shakes, her head jerks from side to side. "A rabid jabber poured from her foaming lips," Lucan writes, "then groans and loud babblings as she gasps to draw breath; doleful howls and wailings fill the cavern." Finally, after the virgin is mastered, Apollo's voice offers the requested oracles. The scene plays out with more frenzied leaping and rolling of eyes from the prophetess. Finally she sinks into a heap, nearly senseless.[6]

Lucan's drama shows us oracular art in a final stage of collapse. No trace of cooperation is left between the priestess and the supernal forces working through her. In fact, the oracular intrusion is so violent that its recipient is driven into temporary psychosis. Personal dignity is annihilated, and we feel pity and revulsion towards the creature who remains.

Nobody would desire to enter a state of prophetic inspiration after witnessing Lucan's scene. And perhaps this was the point. By late pagan times, many educated persons doubted that oracular knowing could live side by side with rationalistic thought. They did not yet dismiss oracles and divinations as mere superstition; but they distanced their everyday consciousness from that entranced, receptive, de-focused state of mind associated with inspired knowing. A separating wall grew up between the personal self and deep psychic processes. As the wall thickened, that which lay on the other looked more and more frightening. Oracular inspiration was imagined as a heedless force that crashed through the gates of rationality and reduced the mind to sputtering babble. Like the heart-crushing Apollo, divinatory encounter could destroy a person. Oracular art therefore was cordoned off from everyday life and handed over to a few specialists whom many consulted but nobody envied.

But Sibylla's form would soon reappear in new, unexpected guises. While pagan intellectuals were banishing the prophetess to the outposts of society, a small group of Jewish and Christian authors were welcoming her with open arms. During the second century B.C.E. Hellenistic Jews living in Alexandria began composing prophetic verses and circulating them as sibylline oracles. Their purpose was to diffuse Judaistic doctrines and teachings among the pagans through a popular means of communication. Paraphrasing from Jewish sacred texts, the sibyl's oracles recounted the creation of the world, praised monotheism, and attacked ancient heathen (especially Egyptian) practices.

Christian authors were impressed by the words of the Jewish Sibyl (as she came to be called), and hailed her as a spokesperson for the true religion. Over twenty of the early church fathers, including Jerome, Augustine, Clement of Alexandria, Justin, Theophilus, and Thomas Aquinas, referred to sibylline oracles or added Christian precepts to their content. But perhaps the most influential of these authors was Lactantius, an African convert to Christianity and a voracious reader of Latin texts. Lactantius announced that he had discovered a set of very old sibylline oracles predicting the birth, ministry, crucifixion, and resurrection of Jesus Christ. While he did not actually quote the verses in question, his statements were widely accepted, assuring the sibyl a place in Christianity for centuries to come. Paintings and mosaics of sibyls can be found in many old churches, and Michaelangelo included several of the prophetesses in his Sistine Chapel frescos.

And what place does the prophetess hold in contemporary Western cultures? Today she is a distant memory, a word that evokes mystery tinged with uneasiness. "Sibyl" is a favorite name to give fictional characters who draw us into their world and then reveal the unnatural or unholy side of their being.

Modern portrayals also tend to sexualize oracular women. In Par Lagerkvist's novel, *The Sibyl*, an oracle-speaker recalls that she had always longed for contact with the Divine. It seemed as though this intense yearning finally brought a god to her. One day, while in an entranced state of consciousness, she could feel his force hurling itself upon her. At first it felt "like a storm of savage heat, rapture, bliss." But soon the experience took a violent turn:

It broke all bounds—it broke me, hurt me, it was immeasurable, demented, and I felt my body beginning to writhe, to writhe in agony and torment; being tossed to and fro and strangled, as if I were to be suffocated. But I was not suffocated, and instead I began to hiss forth dreadful, anguished sounds, utterly strange to me, and my lips moved without my will; it was not I who was doing this. And I heard shrieks, loud shrieks.[7]

This presentation of sibylline experience broadcasts a warning: We may long for the embrace of mysterious forces beyond our understanding, it cautions, but when the Mysterium finally makes contact with us, watch out! The Divine prefers rape to lovemaking. Bliss will turn to agony; the rational mind will be snuffed out; and nothing will remain of personal identity except the shriek. With these fears always in the background, is it any wonder that the farther reaches of psychic life have not been explored more extensively in our era?

Oracular Knowing and Personal Identity

To receive an oracle is to receive guidance, knowledge, or illumination from a numinous source beyond the personal self. From the earliest times, humanity has sought counsel from the voices of nature, messages of dreams, divine arts of divination, and words of inspired mediums. Oracular knowing is the ability to receive and understand such messages. It draws upon intuitive and imaginal processes which are archetypal in the human psyche.

Oracles serve psychological life in profound ways. They bring us into contact with numinous "otherness," thereby penetrating the ego's felt sense of separation. Consciousness is lifted into timeless realms where past, present, and future offer up their images. Since oracles often reveal the broader spiritual meaning of human experience, they help realign personal identity with the larger matrix of all-that-is.[8]

The shadow side of oracular practice is that it can overwhelm the practitioner and obliterate a sense of self. As Lionel Corbett has pointed out in his work on the religious function of the psyche, some intrapsychic structures cannot tolerate encounters with the numinosum. Such experiences have a structure-altering effect which can lead to fragmentation and psychosis in a vulnerable person.[9] Even in their milder forms, oracular ways of knowing can pose a threat to linear patterns of thinking. For this reason they have been feared and reviled in societies that place great value on ego-directed pursuits.

I see the sibyls as figures of wisdom because they avoid falling into an either/or trap when approaching oracular knowing. They neither shrink from the far reaches of psychic life nor lose themselves within it. The sibylline practitioner anchors one part of her awareness in the self-observing ego while another portion opens to vast "Not-I" forces which supersede personal identity. Her skill is not unlike that of the lucid dreamer who can hold together psychically even in the presence of shattering alienness because he possesses more than one reference point.

We may gain additional understanding of sibylline gifts by reviewing Toni Wolff's thoughts on "medial women." Wolff, an early analyst in Jung's inner circle, described a psychic structure which is keenly attuned to "what is in the air" yet cannot easily be expressed. The medial is in between, an agent, a mediator, neither this nor that, a conveyor. She who carries this structural form is immersed in the collective unconscious of her age, animating those psychic contents which urge to be revealed. She is always at risk of being engulfed by collective contents. And she can pose a danger to others if she remains unaware of the powers moving through her. Wolff emphasizes that the medial woman needs to stay anchored in a solid ego consciousness and make a good adaptation to reality. If she uses discrimination and consecrates herself to her unique role as a go-between, she will function as a mediatrix instead of a mere medium. Then her communications will have a healing influence on the culture she serves.[10]

Wolff's observations about medial abilities are useful for individuals of either gender who court oracular experience. Personal stability and common sense are the best companions on any voyage into the trans-egoic. One must also learn not to identify in a personal way with feelings and thoughts pouring through awareness during inspired states of consciousness. Discrimination is necessary in order to sort out which communications should be shared with others and which ones should remain sealed. (We suspect that the sibyls of antiquity preserved their reputations for wisdom by quashing many an utterance!) Providing the ego with a solid base of safety will encourage it to surrender a portion of its hold on the familiar.

Sibylline images in our era seem far removed from visions of that first prophetess who knelt by her sacred spring and chanted inspired verses. But oracular voices can still be heard today. I think of the men and women who raise their voices, sibyl-like, and warn that the green of earth is turning grey, that the living waters are drying up. They, too, cry out from a violated sense of beauty. Indigenous peoples around the world still provide sanctuary for ancient ways of knowing. Like the sibyl, they see realities which are hidden from conscious view. Remarkable individuals may be found in all cultures (usually at the fringes) who welcome the numinous "others" into their personal chambers without fear. If we can carry these voices into the new millennium, then the sibyl will continue to live for another thousand years. And this time she may offer a small smile with her prophecies.

Notes

[1] H.W. Parke. *Sibyls and Sibylline Prophecy in Classical Antiquity.* London and New York: Routledge, 1981. Parke offers the most extensive and scholarly study of sibyls available.
[2] *Ibid.*, 12.
[3] Adapted from Dionysius of Halicarnassus. *The Roman Antiquities*, Book IV. 62, 1-5, tr. Earnest Cary. Cambridge, Mass.: Harvard UP, 1939, 465-6.
[4] Quoted in Mariana Monteiro. *As David and the Sibyl Say.* Edinburgh: Sands and Co., 1905, 119.
[5] *Ibid.*

[6] Lucan. *Pharsalia*, Book V, tr. Jane Wilson Joyce. Ithaca and London: Cornell UP, 1993, 120-121.

[7] Par Lagerkvist. *The Sibyl*, tr. Naomi Walford. New York: Random House, 1958, 49.

[8] Dianne Skafte. "Delphi's Enduring Message: On the Need for Oracular Communications in Psychological life." *Alexandria: A Journal of the Western Cosmological Traditions*, III, 157-175.

[9] Lionel Corbett. *The Religious Function of the Psyche*. London and New York: Routledge, 1996.

[10] Wolff, Toni. *Structural Forms of the Feminine Psyche*, tr. Paul Watzlawik. Zürich: C. G. Jung Institute, 1956.

A Twelve Step Meeting of the Afro-Brazilian Gods

JOHN E. BURNS

Alcoholics Anonymous and its prolific Twelve Step progeny are clearly monotheistic, Christian and egocentric.[1] It is my contention that for the isolated and paranoid narcotic and alcohol dependent from a traditional monotheistic, Christian, egocentric culture, the Twelve Steps are a good place to start recovery. Maybe it is not ideal, but the simple language is universally available and easily establishes communication and possibly a therapeutic relationship, step by step. Some recovering addicts are comfortable within this traditional context, but others contest the extrinsic male "Higher Power" promoting progress towards perfection, even though the Twelve Steps attempt to take the harsh edge off this theology by inserting, "...God, as we understood Him."

Because Twelve Step groups are entirely voluntary, retention rates are low,[2] although it must be recognized that the self-help movement is the financially accessible mass therapy of the moment which has improved millions of lives.

Recovery rates improve dramatically when the alcoholic is coerced into a consideration of the Twelve Steps. Corporations in Brazil are able to mandate the employee who compulsively uses

---

John E. Burns, Ph.D., is a former Roman Catholic priest, a member of Alcoholics Anonymous (A.A.) and a student of archetypal psychology. He is the founder and director of six chemical treatment centers in Brazil based on the Twelve Steps of A.A.

mood changing chemicals to attend a weekly Twelve Step meeting on the work site on company time as a condition for continuing employment, and to do so for as long as two years.[3] This is a highly effective method for curtailing the abusive use of mood altering substances.

Since the participants are not voluntarily present at these work-site meetings they do not suffer superficiality lightly. This is especially true of recovering narcotic junkies who tend to be younger and more intense in their use and recovery. They bear out Jung's observation in a famous letter to the co-founder of Alcoholics Anonymous, Bill Wilson: "...craving for alcohol was the equivalent, on a low level, of the spiritual thirst of our being for wholeness, expressed in medieval language: the union with God."[4] Today, that thought is inherent in the often repeated adage, especially in Narcotics Anonymous: The drug user is on a spiritual quest but knocking on the wrong door.

The strong childhood fantasy of the god "up there" is often the only idea that maintains some proportional presence in the inebriate's addled mind, but as the brain clears, and the fear of life subsides, they seek depth. The need to respond to this search for depth in the chemical dependency treatment centers in Brazil that I am affiliated with has driven us from the position of presenting the Twelve Steps as a singular solution, to the Steps as an over-arching initial position which permits a wide variety of options. We hang out numerous hooks and display an array of possibilities hoping the compulsive substance abuser will see some alternate attractive motivation for living. Intuitively we've shunned egocentric approaches, so most of our counsellors are social workers or laypersons recovering from an addiction, with few psychologists or psychiatrists.[5] People in treatment are considered residents of the community, never patients.

Within this community the mythopoetic labyrinth of archetypal psychology, especially as espoused by James Hillman, engenders a rich, beguiling climate. We hold periodic workshops for staff and other professionals, study the Greek myths and work with images. Since this view of the world requires a Copernican shift and does not settle into an orderly methodology, it elicits much questioning, amazement, awe and considerable incredulity but is fascinating and entertaining with adequate grins, chortles, laughs and outright guffaws.

"Staying with the image" is difficult but residents enjoy working with them through drawing, painting, clay, stories, fables, myths, and poetry, and seldom look for an underlying meaning. They are content to just stay with an image. This evokes emotion, and as James Hillman says, there is value in emotion. The images open new perspectives. They fill the treatment climate with tantalizing, disturbing and seductive hooks that tickle the psychic numbness. We are initially not sure where this is going, but once the gods are summoned, they cannot be easily shaken. *Eh-teos*, enthusiasm is created.

Encouraged by these developments, I carried our experience off to international conferences only to be met with blank stares. Mentioning polytheism bordered on the obscene and insurance companies have gutted the soul of most Twelve Step treatment programs in the USA and Canada. Foreign colleagues who visit our treatment residences in Brazil question how we can maintain such a varied and rich therapeutic climate, although admittedly tumultuous and ambiguous at times.

Part of the answer is in the influence of the omnipresent Afro-Brazilian polytheistic religious practices. The remains of a ceremony: terra cotta bowls with rice, beans, manioc flour and a sacrificed chicken surrounded by colored candles, coins, a black cigar, ribbons and a bottle of sugar cane alcohol can be found on a crossroads corner in an urbane, urban area on any given morning. They are never touched or remarked upon. Rather, they are feared and treated with feigned indifference. The aching wino never succumbs to the divine booze. If a visitor forces a comment, you might hear the Spanish aphorism, *Yô no creo en las brujas, pero que las hay, las hay.*[6]

A closer look at the Afro-Brazilian religions might help establish that polytheism is not only alive and useful in this world, but it can thrive in a predominantly Christian culture and breed a healthy tolerance for ambiguity and paradox.

The Portuguese accidentally "discovered" Brazil in 1500 and immediately occupied it (not colonized it, as the Spanish did) for the mercantile extraction of Brazil wood for red dye and the cultivation of sugar cane, still a major crop. The indigenous Indian population was protected by the Jesuit *missiones* (where Negro indentured servants were used), so an estimated 3.5 million Africans were forcibly imported from all parts of their continent from the 16th to the 19th century as a work force,[7] and to "save their souls."[8]

By the time Napoleon forced the migration of the Portuguese crown to Brazil in 1807, thus establishing the only monarchy in South America,[9] half those included in a census of the new kingdom were in bondage.[10]

Despite the heterogeneity of the slave population, there was some stability which permitted the retention of communal religious practices because: 1) Sugar plantations, unlike mines or cotton and tobacco plantations, employed concentrations of up to one thousand slaves, 2) During the almost 400-year history of slavery in Brazil many slaves became free persons and established their own colonies, 3) widespread and tolerated miscegenation, 4) From 1700 to 1850, the captives exported to Brazil were drawn almost exclusively from the Bay of Benin (modern Togo, Benin and Nigeria), with a common religion and language, Yoruban (*your-U-bahn*).[11]

The Yorubans settled in the State of Bahia, where their religious practices are still flourishing. These same cults are disappearing in their homeland,[12] a region in Africa where the Catholic Church is prospering. Curiously, the Catholic Church is waning in Brazil. It is suggested that the syncretism forced on the black population by the Catholic Church has galvanized integration and growth within the Brazilian culture.

The religious practices that migrated to Brazil have been studied extensively[13] but there seems to be no way of determining just how many sects, nuclei or adherents exist. The city of Salvador, the capital of Bahia with 2.5 million inhabitants, eighty per cent of which is black, is estimated to have two thousand Afro-religious centers, each with about thirty consecrated officials.[14]

Half of Brazil's population of 150 million is considered Negro, second only to Nigeria. Unlike Haiti, the Afro-Brazilian religions thrive in the metropolis. Any major Brazilian city has many hundreds of congregations, but they are difficult to locate. Reacting to years of oppression, they are discrete, tolerant and do not proselytize. Their presence is hinted at by the little stores that sell the paraphernalia for the rituals: candles, incense, imported pigments, chalk, statues, drums, holy waters, perfumes, oils, silks, plumes, beads, stones, gems, cowry shells, herbs, spices, plants, roosters, doves and guinea hens for sacrifice. Most neighborhoods have one.[15] Cities in Brazil are modernly and efficiently electrified but the sale of candles continues to increase.

The diverse Afro-religious associations are constantly adapting, at times melding into spiritism, the esoteric, Amerindian myths and tourism, But gradually the Yoruban *Condomblé (condome-BLAY)* of Bahia is dominating and bringing some order to protect against the charlatan and psychopath, and to develop a political presence.

Amidst the various religions and their derivatives, there are three characteristics common to all the Afro-beliefs. They all have a specific locale for celebrations, anointed leaders and lots and lots of gods.[16]

Plots of blessed bare earth about the size of a volleyball court are fenced off with an altar crowded with statues at one end and a platform for the drummers to one side. They are not called temples or churches but bare earth, *terreiros (tear-HAIR-oohs)*, and are always tread on with bare feet. The area is covered with a tile roof structure which is open on the sides and has benches for the public. The decorations are bright paper streamers, flowers, insignias, signs and symbols, and are lit with many candles. There are also scattered outbuildings and sacred plants and trees. Older assemblies have generations of members living in the surrounding district and take care of their own needy.

Each assemblage is independent financially and liturgically, with a calendar of feasts for the gods of the *terreiro*, which generally coincide with the Catholic celebrations of Lent, Advent, Easter and the days of Saints John, Peter, Paul, Lazarus, Cosmos and Damian, Anthony, Sebastian, George, and All Souls' Day, and Immaculate Conception, but curiously, not Christmas. The governing figure is a mother or father of the gods, responsible for the organization and administration of the *terreiro* and control of the gods when they appear during the trances of the daughters and sons of the gods, the next level in the hierarchy. Lesser in rank is a plethora of minor orders including the drummers, singers, sacristans, cooks, slayers of the sacrificial animals, tailors, seamstresses, a bursar and a master of protocol. Candidates for a vacancy are chosen by throwing the cowry shells for guidance and then initiated into their sacred role. A retired and venerated elder often lurks in the wings exerting his influence and controlling the internal intrigues. At the base are the devotees, much like the members of any church who attend the services and financially support the institution. They span the social and color spectrum, including Orientals of whom there are many in Brazil. Personally requested interventions, initiations and divinations also generate funds. The mothers and fathers of the gods support themselves from the proceeds of the activities, but the others are generally volunteers with outside jobs.

Constant in all the Afro-Brazilian sects is the belief that every person is born with a fixed constellation of gods, of whom one is dominant. It is the special task of the upper members of the hierarchy to determine the principle and lesser divinities of each individual by matching their personality traits with similar personality traits from the pantheon of the gods.

The initiation formalities to enter and advance in the hierarchy of officials is not secret, but still, it is not public. The initiate is isolated between seven and ninety days and has the head shaved. The initiate is then washed in the blood of a goat, pig, rooster or pair of doves depending on his/her predominate god, eats a specific diet, avoids being photographed, wears special clothing and amulets, visits Catholic shrines, and often abstains from sex and undergoes endless purifications. There are recurrent obligations performed in order to maintain the office.

The gods are initially called to the *terreiro* for a festive ceremony by a tattoo from the three long sacred drums, and although their intricate rhythms will vary they continue throughout the night. A mother or father of the gods appears and chalks sacred signs on the ground. Animals are sacrificed and carried off to be dressed and cooked, and, finally, about fifteen daughters and sons of the gods appear in skirts and loose shirts and pants. All the clothing is a brilliant white.

These healthy, graceful dancers twirl in a counterclockwise circle to an increasingly sensual rhythm, singing hymns in a mixture of Portuguese and Yoruban, until one of the dancers falls into a trance. A mother of the gods immediately takes charge, protecting the person from personal injury, verifying the veracity of the altered state by applying a sharp or hot object and examining the pupils of the eyes. She then converses with the god that is appearing to determine whether it is the principle spirit of the person being possessed.[17] If not, the trance is broken off. With her approval the individual is taken to a dressing room, decorated and outfitted with the appropriate, colorful apparel and instruments of the god appearing. These instruments are often a crown, sword, shield, cigar, bow and arrows or a scepter.

In a costume that contrasts dramatically with everyone else in white, the individual is escorted back to the *terreiro*. There are elaborate chants, obeisances, food offerings and conversations between the mother of the god and the god which has become visible. It is during this time that counsels and messages are transmitted to the community. Spectators line up for personal consultation especially if the god present is their dominant god. After everyone who wishes consultation is satisfied, the person is brought out of the hypnotic state.

This sequence of events can repeat three or four times, each with a different god, until the god whose feast is being celebrated appears. At this point the observance is often much more detailed and elaborate. This ends the ceremony. The foods of the sacrifices and offerings are distributed with some cold beer in an informal climate of alleviation and camaraderie of having shared a deep common experience.

The atmosphere during the rites is intense but not dense. It is colorful, sensual, flowing with the changing rhythms of the drums and the chants, always maintaining a careful relationship between the ritual and the space. There is never any overt sexuality or nudity[18] and the only psychoactive drugs present are a little tobacco and alcohol as part of a specific liturgy. The major feasts of the older communities often have a bit more of a dramatic· theatrical effect.

There are few activities at the *terreiro* beyond the initiations and feasts. One can order a special intervention for a specific purpose, but never to bring harm to another person or do black magic. Thus these practices remain on the street corners. Another common sight in all of Brazil is the older, heavy-set black women dressed in immaculate, multi-layered, white skirts offering divination with cowry shells and selling spicy foods with lots of shrimp deep-fried in palm oil.

There are literally hundreds of African gods caught up in elaborate intertwining myths similar to other myth systems, especially the classical Greek, although I was unable to elucidate a reasonable comparison between the two.

Here are a few of the more common gods:

Olódùmaré (oh-LOW-do-mar-EY) is the supreme being above all who created the other gods to govern in the world. Beyond human comprehension, inaccessible, he is indifferent to the destiny of mankind and does not hear their supplications. There are no myths expounding his etiology nor are there cults in honor of *Olódùmaré*. He only intervenes to settle the disputes between the other gods as a court of last resort. Similar to the pietist "absent landlord" notion of the Supreme God at home in heaven.

Êxu (hAY-shoe) is the Trickster. Irascible, ambivalent, obscene and earthy. He causes dissension and calamities, but communicates with everyone and is a good judge of character. The few who have *Êxu* as their dominant god are very difficult personalities.[19] He drinks a lot and is sexually compulsive. Portrayed with horns and a large erect penis, he is often identified with the Devil. Jealous of two farmers he walked between their properties with a hat red on one side, white on the other, which led to an argument about the color of the hat until the farmers eventually killed each other. He is patron of the market place where there is much activity and deceit. His symbol is the trident, his colors are red and black and his day is Monday. Before any commemoration begins he must be appeased with a great quantities of food, liquor and strong black cigars, so he will act as a messenger to call in the other gods and not play tricks.

Oxalá (oh-shah-LAH) is identified with Jesus Christ. In the elaborate Yoruban creation myth which was a real brawl among the lesser gods, one that *Olódùmaré* permitted, *Oxalá* always pulled things together avoiding disasters and guaranteeing the crops. He is the Savior, calm, respected, obstinate, independent and with an iron will. The dancer representing him appears in brilliant white with collars and bracelets of gold and a shawl which is sprinkled with the blood of a white goat or white dove and then washed in special herbs. Few practitioners of *Condomblé* are presumptuous enough to claim him as their dominant god because it would be a great obligation. His day is Friday. He is also syncretized with Our Lady of a Good Death, and her shrines are thoroughly washed once a year by the fellowships in a great public feast in honor of *Oxalá*.

Iemanjá (ee-eh-mon-JAH) the best known of the Afro-gods is the Queen of the Waters, especially the sea. Identified with Our Lady of the Immaculate Conception, she dresses in sky-blue satin and wears a string of pearls, a tiara, a richly decorated fan and a long white veil with gold stars. Her statue, which is the most common artifact of *Condomblé*, has alabaster skin, large breasts and is sometimes in the form of a mermaid. Her foods are corn and fresh young lamb. The dancers that honor her mimic the waves. Her day is Saturday. A strong personality, she is maternal, serious and seeks luxury. On December 31, many millions of Brazilians and tourists with no other connection to the Afro-Brazilian religions dress in white and go to the nearest beach to honor her. Miniature boats painted silver and filled with a bar of soap, a mirror, a bottle of perfume, a comb and white flowers are ritually prepared with much dance and song. At midnight they are launched, accompanied by a massive fireworks display. Copacabana beach on New Year's Eve in Rio de Janeiro is a remarkable scene and worth the visit. If the winds or tide return the boats, a bad year is anticipated.

Ogum (*oh-GOOM*) started out in Africa as the protector of the farmer, but since the slaves had no interest in agricultural production, he became the fearless warrior who unmasks injustices. Associated with Saint George the dragon-slayer, his colors vary but always include the reds of blood. His symbol is the sword and other wrought iron tools. Associated with Wednesday, his food is red meat and palm wine, and his dance imitates the march of a warrior. He is the most prevalent dominant god.

As a white male from the Christian tradition, I can only observe and appreciate this non-linear, polytheistic, poetic set of gods which is so real among its adherents. The Afro-Brazilian mindset, so misinterpreted as shiftless and aimless, contributes richly to Brazil's culture.[20]

Notes

[1] See *Spring 52*, *Spring 58*, and *Spring 59* for a spirited discussion of archetypal psychology and Twelve Step groups. See also Ernest Kurtz, *Not God: A History of Alcoholics Anonymous*, Center City, Minn.: Hazelden Foundation, 1991, for a scholarly presentation of A.A.'s religious roots.

[2] A.A. conducts a careful survey of its membership every three years. See John Bragg, *Comments on A.A.'s Triennial Survey*, New York: A.A. General Services Office, 1990, in which the author demonstrates in Appendix C that only 5% of those who enter A.A. remain after one year.

[3] Not generally feasible in the United States, Canada, or Europe because of laws prohibiting discrimination and the impersonal nature of the work place.

[4] Robert Thomsen, *Bill W*. New York: Harper & Row, 1975, 362. Bill Wilson attempted to provide as broad a theoretical underpinning for A.A. He wrote Jung concerning an early member of A.A., Roland Hazard who had not been successfully treated by Jung in Zürich but subsequently recovered in the Oxford Group Movement (James Buchman), the precursor of A.A. Jung recommended that Roland seek a spiritual/religious solution to his problem.

[5] Of course there is an economic determinant working here; social workers cost less. Also, Jungians are scarce in Brazil, where Freud is still the measure and Lacan is all the rage.

[6] I do not believe in witches, but that they exist.

[7] Roger Bastida. *As Religiões Africanas no Brasil*. São Paulo: Biblioteca Pioneira de Ciências Socias, 1989, 50-74. A curious historic note: Slavery was only abolished in Brazil in 1884, so after the American Civil War, colonies of vanquished Southerners migrated to Brazil bringing the watermelon, pecan nut and sideboard plow as well as a few slaves. The white colonists faded away leaving only a cemetery, while the slaves prospered.

[8] See Pierre Fatumbi Verger. *Orixás*. Salvador, Bahia: Editora Corrupio, 1981, 23.

[9] Dom Pedro II, King of Brazil, an enlightened monarch, was the honored guest at the First Centennial of the United States in Philadelphia. When he encountered Alexander Graham Bell's telephone, which was being displayed as a handy device to summon the servants, he became noted for his prescient observation: "That is going to change the world."

[10] Helo Vianna. *Historia do Brasil*. São Paulo: Edições Melhoramentos, 1977, 7.

[11] See Pierre Fatumbi Verger. *Fluxo e Refluxo do Tráfico de Escravos entre o Golfo de Benim e a Baía de Todos os Santos*. Salvador, Bahia: Editora Currupio, 1987.

[12] Pierre Fatumbi Verger. *Orixás*. Salvador, Bahia: Editora Corrupio, 1981, 7.

[13] The Combonian Afro-Brazilian Library (http://www.ongba.org.br/comboni) was most helpful in preparing this paper and willingly responds to requests for information. The academic raiding, publishing, and thesis writing, especially by the French, of this oral tradition, putting it into a "scientific format," raises the scholar to an unmerited position of authority, dries out the soul, and sanitizes this earthy communing with the gods by rationalizing, classifying, codifying, dogmatizing, formalizing, creating expensive bibles, and worst of all, Westernizing it. There is presently a movement among the academics to de-syncretize it, purify it, and remove the Christian accretions. Do I see available African Studies grants?

[14] Based on an October 1998 interview with Padre Heitor Frisotti, a recognized authority, who willingly replies to inquiries at the e-mail address: comboni@zumbi.ongba.org.br.

[15] I live in the megalopolis of São Paulo, and if I had not been writing this article, I would not have noticed a banner along a main thoroughfare next to a McDonald's near my home inviting all the local Afro-Brazilian priests to a collective baptizing for new members of their hierarchy.

[16] This account was derived from a lengthy interview with a prominent Father of the gods, Jaime Montenegro Sobrinho, in Salvador, Bahia during October, 1996, as well as the following texts: 1) Pierre Fatumbi Verger. *Orixás*. Salvador,

Bahia: Editora Corrupio, 1981; 2) Edison Carneiro. *Candomblés da Bahia.* Rio de Janeiro: Editora Tecnoprint, undated; 3) Vagner Gonçalves da Silva. *Orixás da Metrópole.* Petrópolis: Editora Vozes, 1995.

[17] Participants undergoing the trance report that it is not a pleasant experience. There is a sense of vertigo and losing control. Alcohol consumed in that state does not seem to have any effect and claims are made that nothing is remembered after returning to normal.

[18] Brazilians instinctively and carefully distinguish between sensuality and sexuality, something I do not observe in the United States.

[19] Although a god is designated as male or female, he/she can appear in either a daughter or son of the gods as their dominant god.

[20] The best exposition of this and the key to understanding Brazil is in the work of Roberto Da Matta, a cultural anthropologist at the University of Notre Dame. I especially recommend his book, *Carnaval, Rogues and Heroes: An Interpretation of the Brazilian Dilemma.* Trans. John Drury. Notre Dame, Ind.: University of Notre Dame Press, 1991.

C. G. JUNG IN THE HEART OF DARKNESS

MICHAEL ORTIZ HILL

In 1925 Carl Jung traveled in East Africa. Although he had imagined initially he was involved in a scientific inquiry into "primitive psychology" (the Bugishu Psychological Expedition), he was later to admit that in all honesty his true intent was to pose to himself "the rather embarrassing question: What is going to happen to Jung the psychologist in the wilds of Africa?" (*Memories, Dreams, Reflections*, 272).

During his stay in Africa, Jung had only one dream with a black person in it. In the dream he was with an "American Negro," who had been his barber in Chattanooga, Tennessee, when he had visited the U.S. twelve years previous. The barber held to Jung's head a red-hot iron in an attempt to render his hair nappy. He awoke with terror. Jung took this dream to be a dire warning from the unconscious that he was in danger of being engulfed by primitivity. "At that time I was obviously all too close to 'going black.'"

It is far too simple a distraction to use this essay here to piss on the clay feet of the great man. Throughout Jung's memoirs, one

---

Michael Ortiz Hill is a registered nurse. He is the author of *Dreaming the End of the World: Apocalypse as a Rite of Passage*, which is published by Spring Publications. He lives in California and is married to the writer Deena Metzger.

is impressed by the subtlety and complexity of his mind and the depth of his psychological insight—except when he writes about "the others." The tenacity of his racism, covering five decades of his writings, the radical lack of psychological reflection with which he mistakes his fantasies about the "other" for real people, is embedded in a discourse that is more often than not exquisitely perceptive. His racism raises questions about human ignorance and human wisdom far beyond the personal psychology of Carl Jung because, in spite of, or alongside, his blindness, he was, nonetheless, a wise man. Moreover, since depth psychology has taken the lead of its founding father in interpreting the mythic substratum of human culture, hard questions are raised about the Eurocentrism and racism in Jungian thought and practice.

In a 1977 interview with Jung's autobiographer, Aniela Jaffé, she claimed that Jung's African memories formed the lion's share of what had been edited from their taped conversations to put together the memoirs and that a whole book could have been made from his reminiscences of Africa alone. As it stands, Jaffé was able to whittle Jung's recollections down to twenty pages. Clearly, for the octogenarian Jung, the pilgrimage that was to touch "every possible sore spot in my own psychology" (*MDR*, 273) was still very much alive fifty years after the fact.

That Jung literally regarded Africa as the heart of darkness is clear from his memoirs. The British colonies of Kenya and Uganda were for him that primordial place of time before time, unconsciousness before consciousness, the geography of the primal psyche before it reflects on itself and brings light upon its own nature. Having seen a lone hunter leaning on his spear as his train passed through the outback of Kenya, Jung reflects, "This was the stillness of the eternal beginning, the world as it had always been in the state of non-being; for until then no one had been present to know that it was this world" (*MDR*, 255). Africa was a domain saturated in unreflected light which was at the same time a darkness, a quality of unknowing. The strange statement that no one had been present to know, and therefore bring into being, Africa will deepen in its strangeness as we examine Jung's ideas of the nature of African people. As we shall see, the darkness of Africa's non-being inhabits the dark bodies and souls of the Africans themselves.

To understand how Jung found his bearings in such a dark place, it has to be appreciated how unselfconsciously he inhabited the venerable the old European archetype of the continuous "Chain of Being" that stratifies and holds in order a hierarchical cosmos. Aristotle first articulated the Chain of Being. It is, "as usually conceived, commenced with inanimate things and ranged upward to the lowliest forms of life through the more intelligent animals until it reached man himself; but it did not stop with man, for it continued upwards through the myriad ranks of heavenly creatures until it reached its pinnacle in God," writes Winthrop D. Jordan in *White Over Black*. In the late 1700s the European and American intelligentsia racialized this idea, Jordan continues, to satisfy that "century's ravenous appetite for hierarchical principles in the face of social upheaval." Blacks, of course, being the lowliest of humans, stood in proximity in the chain to their near cousins, the orangutans, with whom, Thomas Jefferson among others believed, they sometimes mated. In the first four decades of this century, another time of overwhelming social upheaval, Jung encoded the "Great Chain" into his model of the collective unconscious. Europeans, being at the pinnacle of evolutionary development, carry within their psyches the whole history of humankind from the "primitive" (instinctual, animal-like) to the civilized (differentiated, European-like). "In the collective unconscious, you are the same as a man of another race. You have the same archetypes, just as you have, like him, eyes, a heart, a liver, and so on. It does not matter that his skin is black. It matters to a certain extent, sure enough—he probably has a whole layer less than you. The different strata of the mind correspond to the history of the races," writes Jung (*CW* 18, 46).

This whole layer that is lacking in "non-Europeans" of course makes all the difference—makes it in fact possible for Jung to understand them better than they can understand themselves.

It was with this map of culture, psyche and history that Jung went to a place that he called Africa, a place that *ipso facto* mirrored perfectly a dark domain of his own interior life.

And the blacks that he met in the "interior"? To illustrate how Africans unreflectively think in feelings and act upon feelings without European self-consciousness, he offers the following anecdote about "a bushman [who] had a little son whom he loved with a tender monkey-love characteristic of primates" (*CW* 6, 239).

It seems that the father had a bad day fishing and when he was met by his little boy at the day's end, he throttled him in pure unconscious rage. Later he grieved with the same "unthinking abandon" with which he had strangled his child.

The opposite of this thoughtless acting out from "instinct" is what Jung called individuation. The individuated person has extracted him or herself from the slag heap of unconsciousness to meet the world creatively, unfettered by personal or collective fantasy. Ironically, the quality of unreflectiveness that Jung attributes to the primitive psychology of blacks is displayed consistently in Jung's fantasies about the "other" . As much as any other European intellectual in the last two centuries, Jung lived unconsciously within the collective fantasy of the "Chain of Being." Indeed, inscribing the chain into psychological theory elevated it from "description" to a sacred way of knowing. When one unreflectively makes the kind of pilgrimage Jung made, the psyche will insist on finding, conjuring or hallucinating an epiphany of darkness that is raw and overwhelming in its terror and vitality.

This inevitable moment came to pass one night during a *ngoma* in the Sudan, a ceremony that Jung took to be a "frolic." Sixty men appeared with lances and swords, and soon the women and children joined them around a blazing campfire.

Looking around nervously, Jung noticed that his "boys" and the government soldiers had disappeared. He began passing around cigarettes and safety pins to demonstrate his good will.

When the men began singing in the firelight and dancing fiercely with their weapons, Jung joined in, swinging his rhinoceros whip above his head. Apparently delighted about the European giving himself over, the dancing and drumming increased in vigor. Jung became frightened that "the dancers were being transformed into a wild horde." He suggested to the chief that it was time to stop and disperse, that it was time for the people to go to sleep. The chief, clearly having a good time, was not inclined.

Recalling the story of another Swiss who had been "struck by a stray spear" during such an event, Jung disregarded the chief, drew the people together, distributed yet more cigarettes and made a gesture of sleeping. That being ineffective, "I swung my rhinoceros whip threateningly, but at the same time laughing, and for lack of a better language, I swore at them loudly in Swiss German...General laughter arose; capering, they scattered in all directions and vanished into the night."

When I read this section of Jung's memoirs years ago, I was struck by its cartoonish quality. I tried to imagine, say, a Nigerian businessman securing a deal in Munich and then going off into the Bavarian countryside during Oktoberfest. Wanting to make a good impression, he passes out the African equivalent of cigarettes and safety pins and even, to the laughter and delight of the crowd, attempts awkwardly to dance a few of the local dances. Late at night, however, overwhelmed by the wild drunkenness of the natives, he appeals to the Burgermeister to rein things in a bit. This failing, he curses at the vigorous young Aryans with mock anger in the *Ibo* language while swirling a whip over his head and laughing. "Capering, they scattered in all directions and vanished into the night"? Well, I suppose some lunacies do not translate across the line that separates colonizers from the colonized.

Whatever the merits of my minstrel fantasy of a black *doppelganger* of Jung in the heart of whiteness, it cannot do justice to this moment once one understands that the *ngoma*, far from being a "frolic," is actually one of the most durable and sacred ceremonies in Bantu culture. *Ngoma* ceremonies, in which the ancestors come forth to inspirit the lives of the living, is probably the most pervasive form of healing and festivity over a rather large portion of black Africa. *Ngoma* is very much at the root of what would become African-American culture, and it is critical to understand if one is to speculate upon a depth psychology of American Blacks that is not Eurocentric. As an initiate into the *ngoma* of the water spirits in Zimbabwe, I find my mind nearly breaking with astonishment trying to imagine this moment as it was viewed by the villagers who had gathered to honor their ancestors. It says something of the forbearance and generosity of African people that Jung wasn't in fact stuck by "a stray spear" that night, given how he was acting.

As terrifying as this dark epiphany was, Jung also discerned in Africans an unconscious yearning for the light, and it moved him deeply. In a pivotal passage in his memoirs, he writes of his habit of waking before dawn to greet the rising of the sun. Having witnessed a ritual by a local Bantu (Elgonyi) people that welcomes the new day and having taken note that a clan of baboons also seem to honor the coming light, he writes, "When the great night comes, everything takes on a note of deep dejection, and every soul is seized by an inexpressible longing for light. That is the pent-up feeling that can be detected in the eyes of primitives and also in the eyes of animals" (*MDR*, 269).

This triptych—Jung, baboon, Bantu people, all swept up in the longing for light—seems to have been tattooed on Jung's psyche. Over fifty years later he would write, "My greatest illumination in this respect had been my discovery of the Horus principle among the Elgonyi" (*MDR*, 274). The god Horus, divine light reborn morning after morning, greeted Jung from his temple in Abu Simbel, Egypt, as he sailed "back towards Europe, towards the future." The Horus principle, he writes, "is a myth which must have been told after human culture, that is, consciousness, had for the first time released men from the darkness of prehistoric times... By following the geographical course of the Nile and hence the stream of time...the journey from the heart of Africa to Egypt became for me a kind of drama of the rebirth of the light." Jung, having made a pilgrimage to that prehistoric darkness, was profoundly touched to see the longing for light in the eyes of baboons and African people.

These two kinds of "Africans"—the bushman who unconsciously strangles his little boy, the noble savage whose love of light holds the seed of potential evolution—share an obliviousness to themselves, and yet they are not beyond admiring. Like Jean Jaques Rousseau, or for that matter Herodotus, Jung often invents an "other" who is simpler and purer, both to illustrate the European burden of being the most conscious of humans as well the what Europeans risk losing. Of himself he says, "I have not been led by any kind of wisdom; I have been led by dreams, like any primitive. I am ashamed to say so, but I am as primitive as any nigger because I do not know" (*CW* 8, 286).

It is possible now to understand Jung's astonishing thought that no one had been "present to know" Africa before he had arrived. Africans, living in the primordial soup of uncreated existence, could only meet unconsciously the splendor of the land that surrounded them.

Jung consistently refers to his fellow Europeans as "we" and presumes that "we" are the bearers of consciousness, writing of "our" special relationship to the created world. Reflecting on the Pueblo Indian belief that their rituals assist the sun in its passage across the sky, Jung had searched in vain for "a myth of our own." His pilgrimage to Africa was a critical turning point in his life because it was on that dark continent (his European-ness revealed to him in contrast to its darkness) where he discovered the myth that is at the root of Europeans' special place in the world: man is indispensable for the completion of creation; that, in fact, he himself is the second creator of the world...without which...it would have gone on in the profoundest night of non-being down to its unknown end" (*MDR*).

I find this vision breathtaking in both its grandiosity and its solipsism. Columbus was merely content to discover America. Had he been Jung, he would have stood alongside God and created it. I don't see here the "cosmic meaning of consciousness" as Jung described this myth of individuation as much as the way colonialism constructs a private cosmos. Having vanquished the possibility of reciprocal exchange within which one might suffer the risk of being changed by another, the universe at large becomes a vast colony of Europe. Martin Buber's criticism of Jung comes to mind: The mysteries of dialogue and reciprocity never enter the picture in such a universe because there are no others as fully human as oneself—at least not in Africa.

It was immediately after his recounting of the *ngoma* incident that Jung writes of the dream with which warned him that he was in danger of "going black." What does it mean in Jung's view to go black under the skin? What is it that terrified him that night?

Jung was quite specific in his collected works about the dangers of white people living side by side with black people. "Even today the European, however highly developed, cannot live with impunity among the Negroes in Africa; their psychology gets into him unnoticed and unconsciously he becomes a Negro . . ." (*CW* 10, 121).

That "the inferior man has a tremendous pull because he fascinates the inferior layers of the psyche" was a spiritual dilemma that Jung believed very much shaped the American (that is to say, white American) soul. "Americans present a strange picture: a European with Negro behavior and an Indian soul" (*CW* 10, 507).

The same unreflective exuberance of spirit that Jung found among African primitives he found among black American primitives as well. He tells the story of having dinner in a stiff New England household. Being served by black servants, he felt as if he were in a circus, and he found himself looking at the dishes for the "imprint" of black fingers. The sheer ridiculousness of the situation inspired Jung to crack jokes which made one servant laugh uproariously. "How I loved that African brother," he writes (*CW* 10, 503).

American laughter ("unrestrained, unsophisticated"), the wildness of the revival meeting, the naivete of (white) Americans so similar to the "childlikeness of the Negro"—these qualities that sit so strangely in whites Jung ultimately found odd but not especially dangerous. "Ultimately the Negro, just because he is a minority, is not a degenerative influence, but rather one which, peculiar though it is, cannot be termed unfavorable—unless one happens to have a jazz phobia" (*CW* 10, 45).

White Americans emerge in this portrait as affable, charming and perhaps slightly imbecilic, first cousins of Europeans. Though they behave somewhat like blacks, they have not gone fully black under the skin and degenerated into moral laxity and instinctuality as Jung himself almost did that fateful night of ngoma in the south of the Sudan.

If psychological theory is a disguised form of psychological confession as Jung claimed it is, what might Jung be confessing in his racist psychologizing? Analytical psychology is not reducible to a simple by-product of Jung's neurosis. Nonetheless, the fear of being overwhelmed by the psyche, by instinct, by the anima, by the shadow, by the female or ethnic "other" is such a persistent theme in both Jung's reflections and his theories, an unanswerable and very Freudian question is unavoidable: What was the moment of being engulfed that led Jung to see himself a potential victim of being overwhelmed by the "otherness" within and outside himself?

In 1925 Jung hallucinated a whole continent of instinctual "others" and called it "Africa." The African "other" whom Jung did not know accompanied him to his deathbed. Like the rest of us, it seems he was wedded to what fascinated him and what he least understood.

Going Black

SHEILA GRIMALDI-CRAIG

Michael Vannoy Adams, *The Multicultural Imagination: Race, Color, and the Unconscious*. London and New York: Routledge, 1996. Pp. 269. Paper.

When Jung went to Africa, in 1925-26, his expedition's "water-bearers, a woman and her two half-grown daughters, who were naked except for a belt of cowries" (as he describes them in *Memories, Dreams, Reflections*), drew more than a glance from his European eye. "They were chocolate-brown and strikingly pretty...fine slim figures...a pleasure for me each morning to hear the soft *cling-clang* of their iron ankle rings as they came up from the brook...their swaying gait as they emerged from the tall yellow elephant grass..."

But, as Michael Adams reminds us in his thoughtful new book on color and the unconscious, Jung said he was careful never to speak to these women. "With a single exception...I never spoke to a native woman, this being what was expected of me. As in Southern Europe, men speak to men, women to women. Anything else signifies love-making. The white who goes in for this not only forfeits his authority, but runs the serious risk of 'going black.'"

Sheila Grimaldi-Craig is the regular book reviewer for *Spring Journal*. She is a former teacher in the Connecticut Public Schools.

The fear of "going black" may sound today like some outdated phrase out of Europe's most racist colonial period, but it is a fear that is surprisingly widespread and, as Adams makes clear, surprisingly contemporary.

The chocolate-brown water-bearers were only the beginning of what Adams calls Jung's "panic attack" in blackest Africa. One night, deserted by "our boys and the government soldiers," Jung was surrounded by some sixty men "martially equipped with flashing lances, clubs and swords" who suddenly danced wildly around their women and children with "vigorous, bellicose melodies, not unharmonious, and at the same time began to swing their legs." Jung says he was reminded of "a nervous herd of wild elephants" he had once seen. He immediately tried to restore his "authority." "As a gesture of good will, I distributed cigarettes, matches, and safety-pins." But none of this diminished the enthusiasm of the dancers, and he soon found himself getting into it. "I swung my rhinoceros whip, the only weapon I had, and danced with them."

As the dance proceeded, things got wilder and wilder. "The dancers were being transformed into a wild horde," Jung said, "and I became worried about how it would end. I signed to the chief that it was time to stop, and that he and his people ought to go to sleep. But he kept wanting 'just another one.'"

Jung swung his rhinoceros whip "threateningly" to get the party to stop, "but at the same time laughing, and for lack of any better language I swore at them loudly in Swiss German that this was enough, and they must go home to bed and to sleep now....General laughter arose; capering, they scattered in all directions and vanished into the night."

In his discussion of this incident, wherein he suggests the problematic nature of Jung's reactions, Adams nicely juxtaposes this passage of Jung with a similar "panic attack" that the French novelist Marie Cardinal once had while listening to a Louis Armstrong concert: "My heart began to accelerate, becoming more important than the music, shaking the bars of my rib cage, compressing my lungs so the air could no longer enter them.

Gripped by panic at the idea of dying there in the middle of spasms, stomping feet, and the crowd howling, I ran into the street like someone possessed."

The Europeans' panic fear of losing their "civilized" identity, of "going black," has long been observed, at least since Joseph Conrad's masterpiece, *The Heart of Darkness*. In trying to address the psychology of this phenomenon, Adams sees the significance of Jung's experiences in this tradition:

> We know what happened to Jung the psychologist in the wilds of Africa: he decided to stay white rather than go black. He epitomizes the fear of the white European that to go black is to go primitive, to go instinctive, which is to go insane, which is to lose his ego—and, Jung says, to forfeit his authority. Rather than become a Kurtz, Jung—or his ego—cracks his whip and shouts a curse in order to disperse the primitives and stop their dance, their trance, his panic attack.

Why couldn't Jung just... let go? Is blackness, for a white European, truly *insane*? To the Jung who once dreamed that a black barber in Chattanooga, Tennessee was trying to give him "Negro hair" by coming at him with a red-hot curling iron, Adams cleverly comments:

> He is having his hair kinked, his thoughts unstraightened. It apparently never occurs to the white European Jung (or if it does occur to him, he resists the implication) that he is, as we say in slang, too "straight": that perhaps he should become "kinky." Perhaps in Jung's dream the unconscious is attempting to compensate his ego's too civilized white European attitude. From a compensatory perspective, perhaps the dream is not warning Jung not to go black—or to think black—but inviting, encouraging, or challenging him to do so.

Jung, as it turns out, has a lot to say about race, color and the unconscious (versus Freud and Adler who, as the furious Frantz

Fanon reminds us, had virtually nothing to say to or about blacks) but before Adams takes all that on he turns to the other side of the coin. What do black people think of "going white"? He cites Michael Jackson's "admission that he had plastic surgery, including a 'nose job,' and his denial of suspicions that he has deliberately gone white by cosmetically bleaching his skin."

And he discusses the first time Malcolm X applied "congolene" (from "Congo") to his hair to straighten or "conk" it. "This was my first really big step toward self-degradation," Malcolm says, "when I endured all of that pain, literally burning my flesh with lye, in order to cook my hair until it was limp, to have it look like a white man's hair." And Charles Mingus, writing in the third person about his own efforts at straightening out the kinks: "Nobody accepted him, kinks or no...The black hate in the air for Whitey was turned on him, a schitt-coloured [sic] halfass yella phony." And Mingus's wonderful conclusion: "He became something else. He fell in love with himself. 'Fuck all you pathetic prejudiced cocksuckers,' he thought. 'I dig minds, inside and out. No race, no color, no sex. Don't show me no kind of skin 'cause I can see right through to the hate in your little undeveloped souls.'"

This is a rollicking book that somehow is able to remain sensitive and empathic with *everybody's* problems and fears. Adams provides story after story, for example, just of the role hair is playing in Afro-American culture today. And he is pretty much up to the minute (if not to Dennis Rodman):

> The variety of hair styles is everywhere evident in the post-kinked, post-conked, cornrowed, dreadlocked diversity of personal and political, private and public statements that African-Americans now proudly make with their hair. I would add that as recently as 1992 I witnessed on the street in New York City a young African-American man cruelly ridiculing an older African-American man for continuing to wear an Afro. As late as 1994, Michel Marriott reports, a new generation of African-Americans suddenly developed a certain nostalgia for the Afro:

> Sharnteek Whitmore, 27, a barber who has been cutting hair for 11 years, said that lately, almost a quarter of his customers at the S & B Barber Shop on Malcolm X Boulevard in Harlem ask for Afros.

Despite the account of a neo-Nazi white supremacist who murdered a Chicago plastic surgeon for "diluting Aryan beauty" with the use of hair dyes and tinted blue contact lenses, Adams is optimistic:

> What we are currently witnessing is a proliferation of hair styles among both blacks and whites. No longer do blacks necessarily style their hair in an effort to look white, and whites now often style their hair in an effort to look black, which, to them, suddenly seems more stylish. The self, whether black or white, adopts, adapts—appropriates—the look of the other. Not only that, but also many blacks and whites are now availing themselves of the opportunity to style themselves in ways that exist nowhere in nature. What 'race' does one belong to if one has blue, green, pink, or purple hair?

But Adams is not at all for eradicating the differences among people. When Jung analyzed fifteen African-American patients at St. Elizabeth's Hospital in Washington, D.C., in 1912, he concluded that the unconscious was universal rather than racial, collective rather than hereditary. These black patients dreamed Greek dreams!

Adams nonetheless thinks he has to correct Jung's (and Jungians') tendency to favor the universal to the neglect of the personal:

> Although all images are personal acquisitions, the experience of the individual in this respect is not idiosyncratic. The individual does not exist in isolation from history, culture, and environment. The images available to the individual at a specific time, in a specific place, are also available to other individuals at that same time, in that same place. A common historical, cultural, and envi-

ronmental context provides an array of images of which individuals avail themselves. Individuals at the same time and in the same place will tend to dream the same images because they tend to have the same history, culture and environment. That is, images—whether unconscious or conscious—have a collective dimension that Jung does not adequately acknowledge. Individuals experience life and the world in typical ways not only because they share a "human nature" but also because they share a history, culture, and environment with other individuals.

He loses me here. Jung and Jungians brought back the universal or archetypal in a civilization immersed in the superficialities of the personal. Adams pays the price of his own eclecticism with what amounts to nitpicking.

Adams would remind Jung (who sometimes uses words like "contagion" and "infection" in this context) of his own observation that white Americans have been unconsciously influenced by African-Americans in the ways they dance and talk, laugh and walk, sing, play, etc. "Although the equation of 'influence' with 'infection' or 'contagion' is problematic," Adams writes, "it is also perhaps instructive, nonetheless." Jung after all had plenty to say to white Americans (and even to white Africans!) about blacks in their midst. He seems to have decided that because whites were in the majority in the United States, they did not face the same "problem" as whites in South Africa. As Adams explains it:

> According to Jung, it is a question of being outnumbered, of being overwhelmed. He suggests that the influence of African-Americans on white Americans is mostly external, or behavioral, rather than internal, or psychical. White Americans may "behave black," but unlike white Africans, they do not run such a great risk of "going black"—that is, "thinking black," and "feeling black." Because they are in the majority, white Americans can afford relative behavioral assimilation, which is very different from absolute psychical identification. If there is laxity in blacks, there is

rigidity in whites. Staying white rather than going black is a defensive compensation against a relaxation of the ego. Just as Jung defended himself from the risk of going black, defended himself against the fear of losing his white, European ego on his trip to Africa, he suggests that white Africans must do the same since black Africans comprise the vast majority of the population. In contrast, white Americans have less to risk, less to fear, merely because the demographics of the United States are different.

Adams does not read Jung as a racist; quite the contrary. It is precisely because Jung viewed human beings as all the same in the depths of the psyche, in the collective unconscious, that the "problem" comes. If skin color matters at all for Jung, it matters not as a racial phenomenon but as a cultural or historical one. History, in this reading, is an accident of images. Jung's "historical layers of the psyche" are historical accidents that happen by luck or the lack of it, says Adams (by way of Claude Lévi-Strauss).

Jung died in 1961, just as the worldwide civil rights revolution was about to commence. Jungian analysts since then have, at the very least, to contend with a different social reality from the one on which their psychology was founded. In this light Adam's book reviews what he calls "the color complex" in the writings of such diverse Jungian figures as Rivkah Scharf Kluger, Edward F. Edinger, Robert Bosnak, Andrew Samuels, James Hillman and others.

What does he say about Hillman? In *the Dream and the Underworld* Hillman revalues black figures in dreams not as representations of social reality (i.e., every kind of white person fantasy of a black person trait, from sexual fertility to music and rhythm, from criminality and brutality to spontaneous revolution and warmth) but rather as imaginal images of death; the Black Man as Thanatos. And in *Inter Views* Hillman, the father of soul psychology, reminds us: "You know it was from the blacks that we got the word 'soul' back into our language."

In his "White Supremacy" piece in *Spring 1986*, Hillman much more importantly claimed that colorism determines racism. The archetypal power of color affects the psychology of those who identify with any specific color. For Hillman it is not merely a matter of a white ego or a white person but of white itself that is so defensive and dangerous. Exclusion of "the other" together with the fear of contamination and infection is, by definition, inseparable from the essential meaning of white. Hence his pessimistic conclusion: racism is archetypally built into people who insist on calling themselves "white."

Adams, following Hillman on this says, "Racism or colorism is such an intractable problem because the very persistence of the white ego is dependent on the maintenance of a color complex that enables whites to define the 'self' in opposition to an 'other.'" Thus blacks represent the unrepressed, liberated, unrestrained, uncontrolled, undisciplined—one almost wants to say un-white—behavior that the white ego had to give up in order to become "civilized." Yet Adams mixes this idea in with some of Hillman's earlier ideas:

> Hillman especially interests me because he argues that the white self requires a black other not in order to perpetuate a defensive ego but in order to subvert it—or at least to revise or "re-vision" it. Although when he says that, for whites, blacks epitomize death, he may seem simply to reiterate a reactionary, racist caricature, Hillman selects death, I believe, because it is rhetorically so extreme, so hyperbolic. The image of the deadly black (in contrast to the images of dirty, devilish, abnormally sexual, lethargic, servile, stupid, cowardly, or evil blacks) is the ultimate anxiety, for it entails the utter demise of the white ego. For Jung, the ego has to "die" in order to be reborn; for Hillman, the white ego has to "die"—be "blackened" (or "go black")—in order to be ensouled.

Adams jumbles the chronology of Hillman's thought and claims that he does not address the black ego. What are whites in blacks' dreams? What if white is your "other"? "Perhaps the reason that Hillman does not pose these questions or attempt to provide answers to them," Adams suggests, "is that the two cases are not symmetrical. Blacks may be Thanatos to whites, but whites, it seems obvious to me, are not Eros to blacks. Even if the black ego might need to be 'whitened' (or 'go white') in some sense, to be whitened would not be to be 'enlivened' (in contrast to the white ego, which needs to be blackened, or 'deadened')." But Adams seems to be confusing black and white colors with black and white people, whereas Hillman had questioned, in "White Supremacy," the use of the very words "black" and "white" for people. An archetypal psychology starts with color and the effects of color-thinking on human affairs.

Adams keeps the discussion out of the cauldron of what is today still called "race relations" where so much writing merely attacks the white majority psychological position from the trenches of the black minority sociological position. (He criticizes Andrew Samuels—whom he otherwise admires deeply—for saying that "we [analysts] should consider expressly allying ourselves with marginal and so-called minority groups." For an analyst, says Adams, such non-neutrality is an illogical *non-sequitur*.)

Adams keeps it all as a psychological discussion rather than fall into the sociology department conventions of "racial" identity politics. It is to individual persons (rather than academic categorizations) that he speaks so reasonably:

> Black separatists and white supremacists are merely the most extreme proponents of a "racial" identity politics. Many others, more moderate, both black and white, also color-code differences in an effort to establish or maintain a sense of identity. The expression "going black" is a historical artifact of racist projections by whites, just as the one-drop rule is [if you have one drop of African ancestry in you, you are black, even though it is estimated that up to 90 percent of African-Americans have some white ancestry]. Although the expression and the rule are patently anachronistic, they nevertheless remain obstinately operative. They evidently serve some unconscious psychological (if illogical) pur-

> pose. An individual identity distinct from collective factors such as 'race' is evidently a difficult (although not impossible) ideal with relatively indifferent appeal. It seems that for many whites and blacks the solidarity of "race" is preferable to the solitude of individuation. Actually, at least as Jung defines "individuation," it is only apparently a solitary project. He states that individuation entails a simultaneous differentiation from and relation to collective norms—neither an identification with them nor an opposition to and opposition from them. Individuation, or truly authentic individual identity, requires a critical evaluation of collective factors—and I would add, an appreciation of ethnic differences as incomparably more significant than any "racial" differences.

Amen to that, though before he finishes, he equivocates a bit and backs off from his masterfully maintained psychological level.

> Although this is a psychoanalytic book, I do not believe that psychological analysis is either the only or the best way to interpret "race," racism, and "racial" identity. I would not "psychologize" these issues—as if psychical reality were primary and social, political, economic, and other realities secondary. Equal opportunity may be a potential, but privilege and deprivation are actualities. I simply happen to be a psychotherapist with an interest in psychical reality.

Here he doesn't seem to realize his own strength, and the very weakness—for how many years!—of precisely the sociological, political, and economic "realities" as they have forced their claim to be the dominant "truth" about racial identities.

Adams is a psychotherapist in private practice and Senior Lecturer in Psychoanalytic Studies at the New School for Social Research in New York. (And I should add a disclaimer, that he is also a member of the Advisory Board of this journal.)

BOOK REVIEWS

Black Ladies: A Review of Two Pictorials

Ommer, Uwe, photographs and Calixthe Beyala, text. *Black Ladies.* Koln, Germany: Benedikt Taschen, 1995. Pp. 180, 200 illustrations. $24.99, Cloth.

Keïta, Seydou, photographs and André Magnin (Ed.), texts by André Magnin and Youssouf Tata Cissé. *Seydou Keïta.* Zürich Switzerland: Scalo, 1997. 130 illustrations, Cloth.

Two very different books, these. The first to hit the office was Uwe Ommer's *Black Ladies.* Open this richly photographed work and staring back from the page are any number of African beauties. Resplendent in colorful headdress and set against native backdrop, these black ladies arrest the gaze with force. "I have seen supple waists, nuances of skin colour, the play of light and shadow, slender figures, languorous or lascivious, some indefinable quality, just below the surface, that seems to come from afar, from the stars, no doubt, bewitching and bewildering" rhapsodizes the Cameroonian poet Calixthe Beyala in her introduction to this book.

Yes, I too, was initially bewitched. Being a White American of a certain age, I remember hearing the refrain "Black is beautiful" in its original 60s and 70s context, and I have been waiting for the popular media to catch up to this fact. And what, you ask, have they given us? On the home front we have Michael

Jackson and family, tributes to the plastic surgery and cosmetics industries, while beamed in by satellite from Africa, thousands of starving children surround the plump, plaintive Sally Struthers. On the surface, *Black Ladies* appears to correct these distortions.

Eventually I became bewildered. Maybe it was the blurb on the inside cover which declares "For the aesthete, Uwe Ommer, the bodies of black women represent the epitome of beauty. His photographs are exactly what they show, no more and no less than a homage to female beauty. And of course that homage is paid in the perfect setting, the stunning landscape of Africa." Archetypalists know that there are no photographs or images that "are exactly what they show." The camera is its own metaphor in that a picture can be read both through the viewfinder and back through the lens at the photographer and the world from which he has come. While the cover blurb feigns some type of photographic objectivity on the part of Uwe Ommer, the opening question posed by Calixthe Beyala in her introduction to this book defensively asks "Why should a photographer from the North not be allowed to celebrate the beauty of Black women?"

Black Ladies can be read as a Northern (white) fantasy of black primordial beauty. A form of exotica as erotica, *Black Ladies* breaks ground as a new genre: African cheesecake photography. It's a Sports Illustrated swimsuit edition without the swimsuits. Although all portraits are a collaboration between photographer and subject, the results will reveal one of two directions: the pictures will tell the photographer's story or the subject's. You can present yourself as you wish to be depicted (your fantasy), or you can "smile for the camera," presenting for the photographer's fantasy. It's called "making love to the camera" in the high fashion advertising world. And that's what this book is: advertising. Uwe Ommer is trying to sell you his ideas about African female fecundity, ripe and ready. It's a sexual Disneyfication which sentimentalizes both the ladies depicted and the "stunning landscape of Africa." *Black Ladies* is a certain fantasy of beauty, prettily packaged and commodified.

Seydou Keïta arrived at the Spring office a short time after *Black Ladies*. Three unsigned photographs in an art exhibition on African art in 1991 caught the attention of French curator André Magnin. After a bit of sleuthing, Magnin found his way to photographer Seydou Keïta in Bamako, the capitol of Mali, and produced this book. Seydou Keïta's main body of work spans the years 1948 to 1977. A cabinet maker by trade, Seydou started out in 1935 on a Kodak Brownie camera and worked his way up. It seems everybody he knew wanted their picture taken. No great art is achieved without suffering, or so goes common thinking. This is how Seydou describes his early days:

> Some of the shots were flattering, others weren't so good ... People weren't always pleased when I showed them the results. That's when things got tough, and everyone wanted to beat me up. You see I hadn't had any training at all.

Eventually he mastered his craft and his father gave him a piece of land behind the main prison in Bamako. In spite of certain problems, Seydou opened his studio there:

> It's a place where no one wanted to live because of the "spirits" that threw stones during the night. Even today if you sleep in that house and turn off the light a great gleaming white horse spirit might appear. You can often hear him galloping by at breakneck speed or you can see him shining in the night.. I myself never had any problem because with the photography there was always a light on.

Seydou's customers, some of whom had never before seen a camera, showed up with all sorts of accoutrements. Wearing their own outfits or borrowing the Western style suits at the studio, they were photographed with the talismans of modernity: sewing machines, bicycles, motor scooters, pens, eye glasses. Seydou Keïta's portraits present people at a crossroads between tradition and modernity. What you get in this book is a collage where one page might reveal "co-wives wearing the same dresses in a printed cloth called 'the jealous dark eyes of my co-wife', (*n'sinè muso nyèden* or *n'sinè muso nyè jugo*) while another shows a "young man in the 1960s wearing European clothes" who "... is probably a member of the Bobo, because of his tribal scar tattoos."

Contrast the people portrayed in *Seydou Keïta* with a new Western phenomenon - the "modern primitive." Modern primitives are the people who are behind the piercing, tattooing, scarification, and dreadlocking craze who would seek to set themselves aside from the prevailing "straight" culture. I've often wondered which tribe these people belong to. It's one thing to be part of a dominant culture in which I can go to the mall and buy any number of Guatemalan prints or Nepalese hats or Kinte cloths. It's all so optional and any one of a thousand choices I can make as a member of my real tribe: post industrial consumer. It's quite another matter to have been colonized by foreigners, to have an outside economic, political order imposed on you. That's not optional. This is, in part, what makes Seydou Keïta's photographs so captivating. His subjects are displaying themselves. They are not having their pictures taken as much as they are giving us a picture of themselves and their times. "It was about then that we began our ancestors' culture," he writes in his forward: Seydou's art is that he serves as a medium for the spirits of the people to shine forth.

REVIEWS

General Reviews

Douglas Gillette, *The Shaman's Secret, The Lost Resurrection Teachings of the Ancient Maya.* New York, Bantam Books, 1997. Pp. 304. $24.95, Cloth.

Shamanism in recent years, at least for some, has moved out of the realm of anthropology and cultural history and into an actual practice in the contemporary world. It is not all unusual these days to come upon people who describe themselves as "shamans," although what they mean by this can vary widely. Douglas Gillette, co-founder of the Institute for World Spirituality, uses depth psychology to explore the dark world of Mayan myths and rituals, articulating in the process a unique kind of shaman-as-artist.

"Shamanism—the powerful psychological and spiritual process for re-creating the cosmos and turning death into life in all the dimensions of Reality—was the driving force behind every aspect of ancient Maya life. It always required that the shaman-creator sacrifice himself or herself, allow himself or herself to be struck by the terrible lightning of the gods, descend into the Abyss, and die in the Black Hole at its center. Death in its many forms—emotional, spiritual, and physical—was the price all creative individuals paid to become 'Lords of Life.'

"'Dying' and ahcieving ecstatic oneness with the creator gods led the shamans to create what they believed were divinely authentic things. Creating dvinely authentic things made one a *halach uinic*—an evolved personality that displayed his or her developed character.

"According to the Maya, all authentic human beings were shaman-creators in one way or another. Becoming a shaman-creator required educating oneself, developing one's skills and natural talents, and being willing to undergo the painful deprivations and self-sacrifices that all creative projects demanded. For the Maya, becoming a shaman-creator was not a luxury—not for those who wished to survive their physical deaths. In return for their sacrifices, shaman-creators built their Resurrection Bodies and achieved an intensity of Being that assured them of eternal life."

Harrington, Anne. *Reechanted Science: Holism in German Culture from Wilhelm II to Hitler.* Princeton, New Jersey: Princeton U.P., 1996. Pp. 309. $39.50, Cloth.

Around the time of the First World War, scientists in Germany began to feel that something was missing from the mechanistic, materialistic, deterministic science that the 19th Century had delivered to the 20th. Some said it was feeling itself that was missing, others a vital sense of life, others called it instinct. Jung, of course, as readers of Spring certainly realize, called it soul. The effort to expand the meaningfulness of science to encompass this larger scope produced a new word, "holism," that lingers to this day (though unrecognizably) in New Age culture, in Europe's Green Party, and even on the Discovery Channel. Holism has, as this book eminently shows, come a long way from its origins in the thought of Hans Driesch, Ludwig von Bertalanffy, Jakob von Uexkull, Constantin von Monakow, Max Wertheimer, and Kurt Goldstein (the last four of whom are particularly examined by the author, a Professor of the History of Science at Harvard). Although Jung is only mentioned indirectly, the book provides an enormously useful background to the cultural mood of his work:

"The new 'holistic' science of life and mind that was to replace the old Machine science was really more a family of approaches than a single coherent perspective. The need to do justice to organismic purposiveness or teleological functioning—to questions of 'what for?' and not merely 'how?'—was central in all cases. Beyond that need was a range of overlapping understandings. Some holism was concerned with finding alternatives to the view of the organism as a mere sum of its elementary parts and processes (what was often denounced as *atomism*.) This form of holism aimed instead to understand apparently discrete physiological processes in terms of their roles in the total functioning of the organism. Others understood by holism an imperative to resist the tendency of the time to treat bodily phenomena and mental phenomena as separate ontological categories (so-called psycho-physical parallelism). This holism insisted instead that the task of a human holistic biology in particular must be to reground he mind in the body and to reanimate the body with the mind: psychosomatic medicine would be one of the most enduring legacies of this second holistic tradition. Still another form of holism emphasized the inadequacy of thinking that the 'whole' could be considered merely at the level of the individual organism. It maintained that organismic processes and behavior only make sense when studied as part of a larger system, whether that system be the immediate lived world of the organism, nature as a 'whole,' or (in some cases) the cosmic logic of the evolutionary process writ large."

Kalsched, Donald. *The Inner World of Trauma*. New York: Routledge, 1997. Pp. 230. $69.95, Cloth, $17.95, Paper.

Completely unbearable experiences (traumas) are handled by the psyche's "self-care system" (Kalsched's phrase) in a fascinating way: the system shuts down. A figure (usually horrendous) then takes over as an encapsulation of the trauma itself, in effect stopping the person from suffering any further by keeping one in a frozen state of pre-trauma innocence. Unfortunately the human spirit remains stuck in this frozen state virtually forever, at the mercy of the trauma monster who will not let it live. Psychoanalysis often progresses only to a point where, on the verge of opening up, the patient is told by the monster to stop listening to the analyst or face terrible consequences (the revived trauma). Kalsched, on the faculty of the C. G. Jung Institute in New York, writes brilliantly of the entire awesome process, taking the reader through much previous literature on the subject, from Freud and Jung to Hillman and Henderson. His own readings of the Rapunzel story, the Psyche and Eros myth, and other fairy-tales, as they apply here, are original and moving:

"The story of Eros and Psyche, told as a short interlude in a longer novel *The Golden Ass*, by the ancient Roman writer Lucius Apuleius, has proven irresistible to Jungian theorists. Erich Neumann adapted the story and was the first to interpret it. He approached the story as a paradigm of female development. By contrast, both von Franz and Ulanov see it as a model for anima development in men. James Hillman sees it as an archetypal drama— a metaphorical portrayal of the longing of the Psyche for Eros and Eros for Psyche, and recently Lena Ross has interpreted the tale as the 'struggle to separate from the collective while maintaining a relationship to the divine.'

"In relative contrast to the above analyses, we will be approaching this story as a portrayal of what we have described as the archetypal self-care system and its 'rescue' (by Eros) of a traumatized innocent ego (Psyche). In this story Psyche's rescuer turns out to be a daimon-lover and, like the tale of Rapunzel, the story describes the healing of trauma as a two-stage process in which the protective, loving aspects of Eros are encountered first and the daimonic aspects later. As the story progresses, both Eros and Psyche must suffer the loss of illusion as a relationship is finally worked out between the reality-bound ego and the ambivalent numinous powers represented by Eros in both his protective and persecutory form. Eros/Psyche, then, represent a dyad much like the witch/Rapunzel, and this archetypal structure defines the self-care system of the traumatized patient with its initial *resistance* to change and ultimate acceptance of change's inevitability (which is part of the human condition)."

Shaw, Gregory. *Theurgy and the Soul: The Neoplatonism of Iamblichus.* University Park, Pennsylvania: Penn. State Press, 1995. Pp. 268. $45.00, Cloth.

When the Christian monks of the fourth century rampaged through the Roman landscape vandalizing the temples of the gods and destroying everything pagan they could lay their ruthless hands on, the last remaining civilized people of antiquity turned to the Syrian philosopher Iamblichus for guidance. The foremost Platonist of his time, Iamblichus took the novel position that what was wrong with the world was not the new barbarism unleashed by Constantine's legalization of the Christians, but a decline in traditional values brought on by too much rationalistic god-talk (theology) and not enough god-work (theurgy). Theurgy was the invention of an earlier generation of Platonists who wanted to adopt the religious rituals of the ancient Chaldaean magi in order to participate in and benefit from the deifying powers of the cosmos. And Iamblichus' theurgy did manage to lead to a few hundred further years of ancient soul work among the last of the pagans before the Platonic Academy in Athens was finally crushed, in 529. While the West wallowed in a thousand years of ignorance, the Arabs preserved Iamblichus's treatises, until the great Florentine Renaissance philosopher Marsilio Ficino, deeply moved by their significance, incorporated them into his own ground-breaking neo-Platonic renaissance. The title of Iamblichus's major work, "The Reply of the Master Abammon to the 'Letter of Porphyry to Anebo,' and the solutions to the difficulties that it contains," was later changed, by Ficino himself, to "On The Mysteries," for mysteries were what Platonism and Greek thought itself had become before Ficino undertook his own enlightenment. That enlightenment has endured. Though Gregory Shaw does not say so, in this lively and readable book, even a masterpiece as pointedly magical as Botticelli's *La Primavera* would not have been possible had it not ultimately been for "the god-inspired Syrian," as Iamblichus was called: "In both traditional and theurgical Platonism the demonic was not an external evil on the fringe of the cosmos, for the cosmos was all-embracing and entirely good. Iamblichus, like Plato, placed the demonic within the embodied soul, the only chaos untamed by the Demiurge. Yet, in Iamblichus's Platonism the purpose of this alienation was made clearer: while Plato's Demiurge gave to each soul a spark of himself, Iamblichus understood this to mean that each soul had the responsibility to perform its own demiurgy, that is to say, its own *theurgy*. The task for every soul was to partake in divine mimesis by creating a cosmos out of the initial chaos of its embodiment. Therefore, the 'demonic' condition of the embodied soul was a *felix culpa* without which the soul could not participate in cosmogenesis, including its own creation and salvation.

Platonists of the second and third centuries c.e. had disowned this confusion of the soul. In direct contrast to the traditional taxonomy, Numenius had shifted the demonic from the soul to the sensible world and both Plotinus and Porphyry followed him. These twin doctrines of an upside-down world and an undescended soul were rejected by Iamblichus, who warned Porphyry that such teachings would destroy their entire way of life, saying: 'This doctrine spells the ruin of all holy ritual and theurgic communion between gods and men since it places the presence of superior beings outside this earth. For it amounts to saying that the divine is at a distance from the earth and cannot mingle with men and that this lower region is a desert, without gods.'"

Zweig, Connie and Steve Wolf. *Romancing the Shadow: Illuminating the Dark Side of the Soul.* New York: Ballantine Books, 1997. Pp. 368. $27.00, Cloth.

This has got to be the most *thorough* examination of shadow behavior that anyone has ever done. The authors, who are practising therapists in California, each presents his and her own shadow stories before undertaking everyone else's—an unusually honest beginning for any book. Connie, who claims to have born out of her father's head, like Athena, saw her own femininity "banished into shadow." Steve, a son of Holocaust survivors, found himself being treated as a "young prince," but one who felt secretly unworthy of the privileges. They discuss all the shields people use to defend themselves from shadow (power, sex, money, addiction), and trace shadow back to family values (with "shadow sisters" and "shadow brothers"). Father's sons and fathers' daughters reclaim feminine shadow, while mothers' sons and mothers' daughters reclaim masculine shadow. But then there are single men's shadows, single women's shadows, dating as shadow-work, the ex-spouse complex and demon lovers, and the shadow at mid-life. The reader soon discovers that everything of substance in life casts a shadow.

"In the famous Greek myth of romance, Eros insists that Psyche make love to him in the dark. Like Eros, many of us want to remain hidden when our passions loosen the reins of the ego's control. We long to know the Other, but not to be known. We ask probing questions, but reply with half answers. In a myriad of ways, we run from being seen and avoid becoming vulnerable, disguised in tight personas and baggy clothes, hiding in sordid addictions and clandestine habits.

And yet, right alongside the urgent longing to know the Other and the refusal to be known is the converse longing: the urgency to be known and the refusal to see. Like Psyche, we open our arms to love but we may not open our eyes. We consent to temporary blindness, giving our sweet love to unknown others, people who are not what they seem, people who become strangers with the light of dawn. Like Psyche, we follow the lead of Eros, god of love—and when we light a candle in the dark, we are shocked at his Otherness."

MARY BANCROFT

1903-1997

PATRON OF JUNGIAN PSYCHOLOGY
AND AUTHOR, *AUTOBIOGRAPHY OF A SPY*

"Facts are not the truth but only indicate where the truth may lie."
> — Clarence Barron, Founder of *The Wall Street Journal*, to his step-Granddaughter, Mary Bancroft, New York, 1920s.

"As an extroverted intuitive, power is your natural element. Men seeking or holding power will cherish your advice."
> — C. G. Jung, to his patient, Mary Bancroft, Zurich, 1930s.

"It should work out very well. We can let the work cover the romance—and the romance cover the work."
> — Allen Dulles, founder of the Central Intelligence Agency, to his lover and newest spy, Mary Bancroft, Bern, Switzerland, World War II.

Parker Institute:
A CENTER FOR SPIRITUALITY
1130 Nashville Avenue • New Orleans, Louisiana 70115

"The Institute's purpose is to provide programs through which people explore different avenues of soulful spirituality, cultural enrichment and continuing education."

Sampling of Fall '97 & Spring '98 Schedule at Parker

Stephen Aizenstat, Ph.D., *Presentation and Workshop,* October 3-4
Dr. Aizenstat is the founding President of Pacifica Graduate Institute and a clinical psychologist. Dr. Aizenstat has conducted dreamwork seminars for over 20 years throughout the United States, Europe and Asia.

Ginette Paris, Ph.D., *Presentation and Workshop,* October 30 and November 1
Dr. Paris was a Professor at University of Quebec, Montreal. Currently, she serves as a psychologist and core faculty member at Pacifica Graduate Institute. She has authored books on Greek and Roman mythology, including *Pagan Grace* and *Pagan Meditations*.

Lionel Corbett, M.D., *Presentation and Workshop,* February 13-14
Dr. Corbett is a British psychiatrist and Jungian analyst, and core faculty member of Pacifica Graduate Institute. His most recent book is *The Religious Function of the Psyche*.

Matthew Fox, Ph.D., *Presentation and Workshop,* April 24-25
Dr. Fox is editor-in-chief of Creation Spirituality Magazine and President of the University of Creation Spirituality. He is author of seventeen books including *Original Blessing, The Coming of the Cosmic Christ*.

And many other programs . . .

"Our programs are interdisciplinary, integrating theology, psychology, mythology, literature and the arts. We hope you can join us!"
W. Craig Gilliam, Director

For more information, please call (504) 895-1222

• inhale • a lift • exhale • what to do • inhale • fear

James Hillman
&
Thomas Moore

On Inspiration

**A Rare Joint Appearance
November 8-9, 1997
Chicago, Illinois**

Can we learn to be more receptive to inspiration, with all its fears and pleasures? Can we design more breathing room in our lives?

Join these best-selling authors and renowned psychologists for a weekend of conversation on the workings of inspiration in their lives -- and ours. Be part of a lively exchange where the nature of inspiration, the very life-breath of body, mind and soul, is explored and perhaps glimpsed.

**For more information, call: *1-708-442-2670*
or e-mail: *Bsrc@aol.com***

This event is a benefit for Spring Publications.

• work is done • inhale • in whose service • exhale •

SPRING AUDIO

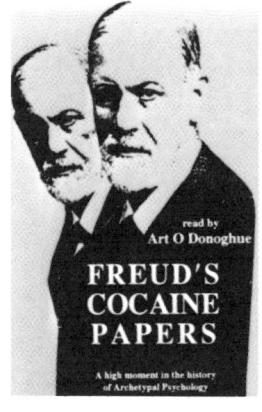

Art O Donoghue
Freud's Cocaine Papers
One Tape: 1 1/2 hrs $11.95

Robert Louis Stevenson used cocaine to overcome writer's block (and then wrote *Dr. Jekyll and Mr. Hyde*), and President Grant used it to write his best-selling memoirs. These are only a few of the tales in this rollicking account of Sigmund Freud's association with the drug, and the events that led to his writing of the now classic "Cocaine Papers." Art O Donoghue and James Hillman rediscovered Freud's papers in Vienna and had them translated for the first time in 1963. In the first part of the tape, Donoghue tells you all about it in a talk recorded live at the Notre Dame Festival of Archetypal Psychology in 1992. In the second part, Donoghue reads selected excerpts from the "Cocaine Papers" which show that their main value is not pharmacological but psychological.

Thomas Moore
Soul and Everyday life
Two Tapes: 2 1/2 hrs $19.95

Thomas Moore's book, *Care of the Soul*, has been on the New York Times bestseller list for months. A practical guide to finding the soul in one's life, he senses the sacredness in ordinary things and shows how to care for it. On this tape Moore takes the listener through a workshop weekend on the soul conducted at the Open Center in New York, where he discusses his ideas on work, money, futility, creativity — what he calls the economics of soul. Moore is a master at getting soul out of Church and back into the Twentieth Century — as the bestseller lists now confirm.

SPRING PUBLICATIONS

Hell, The Underworld, Trauma, Darkness, Disease—and all their cousins

Greg Mogenson's *God Is a Trauma: Vicarious Religion and Soul-Making* brings religion and psychology together by presenting a theology of soul, rather than of the spirit. Faithfulness to the soul shifts our focus from the overwhelming nature of whatever functions as "God" to the small scale of daily soul-making. (167 pp., 0–88214–339–5)

Robert Bly writes of "The Age of Endarkenment" from *Letters at 3AM* that Michael Ventura "has written the greatest essay yet by a member of his generation." Andrei Codrescu says these essays "brilliantly diagnose our fin-de-siecle." Read this book to be "enlightened and enlivened" (Thomas Moore) about our collective psychic and political condition. (247 pp., 0–88214–361–1)

Impossible Love: Heresy of the Heart, by Jungian analyst Jan Bauer, addresses the vertical movement up into the heights and down into the Underworld of betrayal, taboos, and excess that characterizes tragic romances. The 12th-century passion between Heloïse and Abelard and a 20th-century woman's "relationship failures" provide case histories of these experiences that change lives forever. (204 pp., 0–88214–359–X)

Eugene Monick's *Evil, Sexuality, and Disease in Grünewald's Body of Christ* passionately attends to the sickly Christ on the cross of the Isenheim altarpiece. The (sexually?) diseased God-image offers compassionate relief to the burdens of personal guilt and shows the strange beauty shining through the disgust and unbearable pain of pandemic disease. Foreword by David L. Miller and color plates. (189 pp., 0–88214–356–5)

Get 'em while they're cold ...

Spring 53 **(Pagans, Christians, Jews):** Jung's secret initiation into Mithraism. James Hillman on "How Jewish is Archetypal Psychology?" Oracles. Disability. Vampires.

Spring 54 **(The Reality Issue):** Wolfgang Giegerich on killing for consciousness. Edward S. Casey on Reality. Automatic Writing. Hillman's updating of "Alchemical Blue."

Spring 55 **(The Issue from Hell):** Sheila Grimaldi-Craig's "Whipping the Chthonic Woman." "The Children of Hell." Max Nordau's *Degeneration*. "Reading Jung Backwards."

Spring 56 **(Who Was Zwingli?):** Hillman's "Once More into the Fray" takes on Wolfgang Giegrich. Benjamin Sells on Lawyer's Ethics. David Miller on Joseph Campbell. Jung's *Zarathusthra* Seminar, and the first Index to *Spring* in years!

Spring 57 **(Archetypal Sex):** Rachel Pollack on Transsexuals. Hillman on Pornography. John Haule on Erotic Analysis. Sonu Shamdasani on who really wrote Jung's memoirs.

Spring 58 **(Disillusionment):** Joseph Landry on Alcoholics Anonymous, Connie Zweig on Transcendental Meditators, David L. Hart on meeting Jung for the first time, James Hillman on the need to falsify or disguise the story of your life.

Spring 59 **(Opening the Dreamway):** Robert Duncan on what Jung and Hillman meant to his poetry, Nor Hall on Robert Duncan and Jess, Charles Boer on how Gods guide the minds of poets ancient and modern, James Hillman on heroes, Michael Adams on why Jungians hate semiotics.

Each issue is still available (for $17.50) but to subscribers (or renewers) they're only $12 each.
Get all 7 (while they last) for just $60 — a savings of $24!
We pay postage and shipping worldwide :

**Spring Journal
Box 583
Putnam, CT 06260**